D0948497

Collage of Dreams

Works by Anaïs Nin

Published by the Swallow Press
D. H. Lawrence: An Unprofessional Study
House of Incest (a prose poem)
Winter of Artifice
Under a Glass Bell (stories)
Ladders to Fire
Children of the Albatross
The Four-Chambered Heart
A Spy in the House of Love
Solar Barque
Seduction of the Minotaur
Collages
Cities of the Interior
A Woman Speaks
Anaïs Nin Observed (by Robert Snyder)

Published by Harcourt Brace Jovanovich
The Diary of Anaïs Nin, 1931-1934
The Diary of Anaïs Nin, 1934-1939
The Diary of Anaïs Nin, 1939-1944
The Diary of Anaïs Nin, 1944-1947
The Diary of Anaïs Nin, 1947-1955
The Diary of Anaïs Nin, 1955-1966
A Photographic Supplement to the Diary of Anaïs Nin
In Favor of the Sensitive Man and Other Essays
Delta of Venus: Erotica by Anaïs Nin

Published by Macmillan
The Novel of the Future

Published by Magic Circle Press
Waste of Timelessness (stories)

Collage of Dreams :

The Writings of Anaïs Nin

Sharon Spencer

THE **SWALLOW PRESS** INC.

CHICAGO

PS
3527
I865
Z93

Copyright © 1977 Sharon Spencer
All Rights Reserved
Printed in the United States of America

Published by
The Swallow Press Incorporated
811 West Junior Terrace
Chicago, Illinois 60613

First edition
First printing

LIBRARY OF CONGRESS CATALOG CARD NUMBER: 77-78781
ISBN 0-8040-0760-8

Excerpts from *The Diaries of Anaïs Nin* edited by Gunther Stuhlman, copyright © 1966, 1967, 1969, 1971, 1974, 1976, by Anais Nin. Reprinted by permission of Harcourt Brace Jovanovich, Inc.

Excerpts from *The Novel of the Future* by Anais Nin copyright © 1968 by Anais Nin. Reprinted by permission of Macmillan Publishing Co., Inc.

Dedicated in loving admiration to
Anna Balakian
and to
Inge Bogner
and to all the
daughters and sons of Anaïs

Woman will discover the unknown. Will her world be different from ours? She will discover strange, unfathomable things, repulsive, delicious. We shall take them. We shall understand them.

Arthur Rimbaud, 1871

Contents

The Art of Ragpicking

There is no separation between my life and my craft, my work. The form of art is the form of art of my life, and my life is the form of the art. I refuse artificial patterns. Stories do not end. A point of view changes every moment. Reality changes. It is relative.

—*The Diary of Anaïs Nin, Volume IV*

Anaïs Nin is often imagined to have been a wealthy, expensively dressed woman, yet the truth is that many times she remade her clothes or wore dresses purchased from thrift shops. In the Diary she tells of transforming an inexpensive suit or dress into elegance simply by changing the buttons. Seemingly irrelevant, these examples of Nin's thrift actually point to one of her most characteristic attributes: the desire to go about collecting odds and ends; to restore meaning to what has been neglected and to give meaning to what has been ignored or derided. In short, Nin is a ragpicker of experience. And from the rags, debris, and especially from the broken fragments she has gathered up, Nin has made a large body of highly inventive books.

The essential motivation in Nin's life and art is a passionate desire to transform every thing, every experience, and every person, into a meaningful and valuable, if not actually a beautiful, entity. To use an unpretentious phrase, her art might be regarded as a vast reclamation project. To use a metaphysical term, it is an ongoing experiment in poetic alchemy. "Creation is an *alchemy*," she has written.[1] Alchemy is perhaps Nin's favorite metaphor for the process through which art transforms the ordinary into the extraordinary.[2]

1

Nin devoted her life to developing a poetic prose and to inventing structures that facilitated the transformation of her experience into something precious. Precisely because, as she herself said, there is "no separation" between her life and her work, because she succeeded in blending the form of her art with the form of her life and because she rejects "artificial patterns,"[3] Nin inadvertently presents a problem for traditionally oriented readers. They do not know *what* she is writing: poetry; prose; memoirs; autobiography. Unable to fit her books into historical literary categories, too many readers and even critics dismiss them as inept. An essential aspect of the originality of Nin's books is that none of them fit traditional descriptions of literary genres. Her novels are more like sustained poems than fiction. They are feats of improvisation in an imagistic prose that renders character with psychological brilliance. Nin's Diary is not a conventional diary, a spontaneous personal record, nor is it fiction, even though the heightening of event and character, with certain disguises of actual persons, brings this Diary intriguingly close to autobiographical fiction. Anaïs Nin's literary criticism, too, refuses categorization. Although her "unconventional" study of D. H. Lawrence ignores the formalities of scholarship, it is a remarkable achievement of impressionistic criticism and is still today one of the most perceptive commentaries on Lawrence's writing. *The Novel of the Future* is also difficult to categorize. Rich with comments on novels and films that clearly detail Nin's convictions about writing, this book flows beyond the boundaries announced by its title into the realms of psychology, personal growth, aesthetic experience and drugs, the nature of consciousness and of the self. It is a compendium of all the themes that have absorbed Nin's attention since she began writing. Anaïs Nin is not willfully misleading about her literary aims; she is, though, a rigorously independent and self-committed writer whose determination to express a private vision in literature links her to the great moderns, particularly to Proust, and to the discoveries in science and technology that were so richly suggestive for writers during the first three decades of the century.

Nin's assertion "I refuse artificial patterns" implies that for her the "artificial" is that which already exists, having been brought into being by someone else in order to fulfill someone else's expressive needs. "Artificial patterns" are imposed by authorities, patriarchs, priests, or critics who are committed to the protection and promotion of the traditional. In life and in art, Nin has rejected these figures of authority in order freely to create the patterns of feeling, thought, or expression that have seemed to her authentic when measured by a strictly personal intention.

Always rebelling, always improvising, inventing, struggling to translate everything she has experienced into creative work, Nin has, quite understandably, made the artist her hero. In this she echoes the Symbolists but especially Rimbaud's view of the artist as seer, prophet, *voyant*. She views art as one of the few meaningful activities of modern life. In this, as in much else, Nin is allied with Proust and countless other moderns who believe that, with the decline of the power of religion to sustain the sense of the mysterious, artists have inherited the powers that in previous ages were reserved for priests. These include the objectification of spirit in artistic forms; the task of providing man with inspiration to pursue his highest self; the redemption of the irrational; and the metamorphosis, through the alchemy of art, of the dross or base into a substance that is valuable and shimmering, golden, if not gold.

Nin's lifelong struggle has been the creation of herself as artist; this is the battle that is narrated in the six published diaries. Her characters are usually artists. Besides Proust, the one wholly satisfactory, wholly admirable and always delightful person to appear in Nin's books is Jean (Janko) Varda who, in 1944, sent her a collage called "Women Reconstructing the World." The pages of *Diary IV* that describe Nin's visit to Varda in California are radiant. They crackle with the energy that Nin, discovering in the man, transformed into her description of him. Varda "concealed his sorrows." "He delivers us from the strangle hold of realism, the lack of passion and wit of other painters. He fulfills the main role of the artist, which is to transform ugliness into beauty." Above all, Varda "is in a state of grace with love and joy. He extracts from experience only the elixir of life, the aphrodisiac of desire."[4] The only female

artist who is as fully self-possessed and as joyous as Varda is
Renate, the painter. She appears in *Diary V* and in *Collages,* the
experimental book of 1964 whose theme emerges from the presence
of the artist, Varda himself, in his magic role as the wizard who
transforms ugliness into beauty. When someone suggests that Varda
make a portrait of Renate, he declines, explaining that she is
" *'femme toute faite.'* " Varda adds, " 'A woman artist makes her
own patterns.' "[5] The very lack of pre-existing themes and techniques leaves a woman artist entirely dependent on her personal
resources; she is forced to invent the "feminine" for herself.

The fact that Varda is a collage-maker is extremely important.
Collage as a concept underlies Anaïs Nin's sense of art, both in
theory and as process. In fact, collage is, as Max Ernst has said,
"visual alchemy."[6] The idea of collage is central to Nin's expression
of the modern spirit, so brilliantly prophesied by Guillaume Apollinaire in 1918 in his famed essay "The New Spirit and the Poets"
("L'Esprit nouveau et les poëtes"). Here Apollinaire alluded to the
electronic inventions that would transform the twentieth-century
arts. He stressed the importance of the element of surprise as the
"greatest source of what is new," and presented a description of the
collage process. "There are a thousand natural combinations that
have not yet been composed. Men will invent them and put them to
a good purpose, composing with nature that supreme art, which is
life. These new combinations—these new works of art—they are
the art of life."[7] Apollinaire saw that the new could be made from
the old simply by changing the types of elements brought into the
composition, by using scraps of incomplete elements, or by combining familiar materials in unfamiliar ways.

Max Ernst and Louis Aragon, both of whom were connected
alike with Dada and Surrealism, have written of collage and both
stress the magic of this process. In *Challenge to Painting,* Aragon
repeatedly praises collage for its ability through "extraordinary displacement" to achieve the realization of the miraculous (an aim of
Surrealism). For him collage is "black magic," for it leads the
painter "toward the magic practices which are the origin and justification of plastic representation, forbidden by several religions."

Ernst, the discoverer of frottage, photomontage, and a brilliant exploiter of collage technique, declares, "He who says collage, says the irrational."[8] For the Surrealists collage possesses the power of transforming its components into something altogether new and marvelous. Through "alchemy," dross elements are turned into a precious substance by the persistent art of the black magician, the prestidigitator, the Surrealist.

There is a particular sense in which Anaïs Nin's art is related to the Surrealist ideal of magical creation through combinations of entities drawn from different categories. But her work is not itself Surreal, and it is easier to understand the application of the collage idea in terms of a broad definition. Collage includes all works in which components belonging to separate intellectual or perceptual categories are combined, regardless of the nature of the materials or the techniques used to combine them. Collage admits of endless variables. That is why Apollinaire was struck by its power to create the new. Moreover, the possibility of variety is extended because collage includes two types of materials: the ones collected for the composition and the means of fastening them together.[9]

The degree of novelty, shock, or surprise sparked by a collage will depend upon the degree of dissimilarity of its elements. The more "extraordinary the displacement," to quote Aragon again, the more shocking the effect on the audience. The more shocking, the more likely the work will be described as "Surreal." If the degree is relatively slight, the composition may merely seem somewhat off-beat or strange, intriguing the reader with a relatively small tremor of surprise. [10] The degree of displacement in Anaïs Nin's writing is relatively slight, even though there is considerable variety among her works. Her most experimental book, the one in which displacements are the greatest, is *Collages* itself. The early books, *House of Incest* and the pieces collected in *Under a Glass Bell,* display juxtaposition less in a structural sense than in stylistic combinations. Nin's diction is based on collage; she chooses words from a wide variety of sources and is usually successful in achieving a striking yet authentic image, phrase, or descriptive passage. A lover of words *as* words, Nin uses them if they appeal to her, regardless of standards of usage; she also draws upon far-flung vocabularies. "You can go into any number of sources. I draw from paintings, mobiles, scientific journals, dictionaries, films, plays, cities."[11] Guided by the unpredictable lure of free association, Nin combines into a novel the incidents that seem most strikingly to project her characters' inner lives. In *The Novel of the Future* Nin describes how she wrote *Collages:* "I allowed myself to live out a mood and see what it would *construct* [italics mine]. Once the mood is accepted, the mood makes the selection, the mood will give fragments a unity, the mood will be the catalyzer. And so this book, which should have been a novel or another book of short stories, became something else, a collage."[12]

Like Anaïs Nin's fiction, her Diary is also a collage composition. The assembled elements are the bits and pieces of her life: fragile evocations of her feelings; her victories over herself; her occasional moods of despair; richly detailed portraits of the people who moved her, inviting friendship and compassionate analysis, or provoking her disapproval and critical analysis; passages from books and letters; passionate declarations of her aspirations as a writer; passages brilliantly describing the psychological problems of the artist; sharp observations of the cultural patterns of America; and fascinating accounts of Nin's own repeated journeys into psychoanalysis. Selected from the mass of materials of the unpublished diary, the passages that comprise each published volume are themselves a collage composition presenting a phase in the life of their creator.

Nin's Diary, a work of art in itself, possesses special importance for those who are intrigued by the creative process. Because this Diary exists, we can see exactly how Nin's fiction was made. Even greater insights may someday be available to those who are able to study the unedited manuscripts. But a comparison of the present version of the Diary with the fiction reveals first, and perhaps most strikingly, Anaïs Nin's insistent need to preserve her experience, the stuff of her life, by recording it with astonishing dedication, even passion. The intensity and power of this need explains why Henry Miller and Otto Rank were unsuccessful in their attempts to free Nin of the diary. The diary *was* her life, her inner life, which the circumstances of her outer life prevented from receiving full expression. This need to preserve her experience, to protect it from alteration, change, or loss, proves the depth and strength of Anaïs Nin's creative will and inadvertently demonstrates one of the theories of her most famous analyst, Otto Rank.

Rank is very convincing when he argues that the fear of death is an important characteristic of the creative or productive personality:

> There is . . . a double sort of fear: on the one hand the fear of life which aims at avoidance or postponement of death, and on the other the fear of death which underlies the desire for immortality. According to the compromise which men make between these two poles of fear . . . there will be various dynamic solutions of this conflict . . . For, in practice, both in the neurotic and in the productive type—the freely producing and the thwarted—all the forces are brought into play, though with varying accentuation and periodical balancing of values. In general, a strong preponderance of the fear of life will lead rather to neurotic repression, and the fear of death to production—that is, perpetuation in the work produced.

Anaïs Nin has insisted upon carrying out the project of the diary, one that not only embodies her life, but also possesses the very important potential for outlasting it. "The mistake," Rank wrote, "in all modern psychological biography lies in its attempt to 'explain' the artist's work by his experience, whereas creation can only be made understandable through the inner dynamism and its central problems. Then, too, the real artist regards his work as more important than the whole of life and experience, which are but a means of production—almost, indeed, a by-product of it."[13]

In Nin's case there is a special dimension of this creative drive that relates it specifically to collage composition: the desire to redeem experience. " 'I stand for hours watching the river downtown. I look at the dead flowers floating, petals completely opened, the life sucked out of them, flowers without pistils. Punctured rubber dolls bobbing up and down like foetuses. Boxes full of wilted vegetables, bottles with broken tops. Dead cats. Corks. Bread that looks like entrails. These things haunt me. The debris. When I watch people it is as if at the same time I saw the discarded parts of themselves.[14] Characteristically, when Anaïs Nin visited a ragpickers' village on the outskirts of Paris, she found "touching" all the "mismated" and "unmated" objects. Her response to this scene of poverty and devastation was to proclaim: "I could write here."[15]

"Ragtime," first published in 1938, is a dream piece, a symbolic enactment of the artist's reclamation project. Like Varda who says, " 'I'm only looking for fragments, remnants which I can co-ordinate in a new way,' " Nin's ragpicker "never looked at anything that was whole.[16] His eyes sought the broken, the worn, the faded, the fragmented. A complete object made him sad. What could one do with a complete object?"[17] As Rank has said, experience serves the creator. A complete object may be a fine thing within its own frame of reference, but it is of no use to the artist.

As the dream of "Ragtime" progresses, the dreamer gradually becomes identified with the ragpicker, who, of course, represents the artist. He wanders about a garbage dump packing his "swelling" (pregnant) bag with irresistible junk. The dreamer enters this landscape as a passenger on the hump of a camel that is itself only the ragpicker's shadow. Later, as she strolls through a plateau of shacks, gypsy carts, and trash, the dreamer grows increasingly anxious because of the squalor of the scene. "Inside the shacks rags. Rags for beds. Rags for chairs, Rags for tables. On the rags men, women, brats. Inside the women more brats. Fleas." The highly suggestible dreamer, imagining that she herself may come apart, explode into fragments, begins to clutch parts of her body to make sure she is intact. She stumbles upon discarded parts of her self. First, an old dress, once a favorite. But the dreamer has grown, and when she puts on this dress, she can no longer "stay inside of it." Next she finds castoff parts of her body. A wisdom tooth. Her long hair. Naturally the dreamer is disturbed by the reappearance of these parts of her former self. Do they mean that it is impossible to get rid of the old self, to shed one's skin? " 'Can't one throw anything away forever?' "[18]

The ragpicker answers this wistful question by leading his colony of vagabonds in the "serpentine song":

Nothing is lost but it changes
into the new string old string
in the new bag old bag
in the new pan old tin
in the new shoe old leather
in the new silk old hair
in the new hat old straw
in the new man the child
and the new not new
the new not new
the new not new[19]

With this reassuring lullaby in her ears, the dreamer falls asleep (in her own dream), only to be picked up along wth other odds and ends of scrap and stashed away inside the ragpicker's bag (now suggestive, as well, of the sandman's pack). But the reader does not worry about the fate of this particular dreamer. He knows that she will be well used.

Collages, published in 1964 twenty-six years after "Ragtime," is a superb example of how an inventive writer can adapt a technique from the visual arts to literature, in this case fusing a variety of apparently unrelated materials into a striking composition. A more ambitious, a deeper book than its easy surface and gentle humor suggest, *Collages* is composed of nineteen short blocks of prose, beginning and ending with the same passage. This circular structure contains some twenty-two characters in an abundance of quickly sketched settings that range from Mexico to Europe and include California and New York City. *Collages* gives the impression of having been put together from Nin's writer's scrap bag, conceived from the energy of her determination to create something interesting out of her leftover characters, situations, and settings. Again, she wants to use everything. The cement that binds these colorful remnants is Renate, the painter whose portrait Varda did not want to attempt because of her completeness as a woman artist who "makes her own patterns." Renate is the strongest and the happiest of Anaïs Nin's women characters. She weaves in and out of the lives of the others, bringing silent inspiration. Renate is a dynamic example of the artist who sustains balanced relationships to her painting, to her friends, and to herself.

Although Renate dominates the design of *Collages,* her strong and bright area is balanced by Varda, with his tremendous energy and self-assurance. The portions that concern his life and his creations—so brilliantly evoked by Nin's descriptions—are exactly in the center of the book. And rightly so, for Varda's philosophy is the thematic core, teaching the need for beauty and how to achieve it by piecing together the splendid, life-enhancing visions that are called collages. Eventually, even Varda's rebellious teenage daughter succumbs to his spell. She gives up dirty jeans and sweatshirts in order to dress herself in "Varda's own rutilant colors."[20]

Collage art, like all art, works magic transformations. In this book Anaïs Nin repeatedly shows fantasy and dream enriching life, providing the loves that a narrow "reality" denies, dissolving the boundaries between the natural and the perverse, the impossible and the marvelous, comforting and reassuring the lonely and the isolated. There is an intense relationship between a girl and a raven. One character feels more akin to seals than to human beings, and he finally develops the courage to renounce people in order to be with the animals he loves. A gardener experiences delight by pretending to be a millionaire with funds to back a literary magazine. A woman who has lost her husband to a young girl replaces him with an exotic phantom lover, Shumla, a hero of Islam. In *Collages* imagination is sovereign.

The magic of intimate relationships balances the magic of art. *Collages* ends with the reluctant emergence of a woman writer from a bitter, self-imposed isolation. Judith Sands allows herself to be "courted" by Renate and an Israeli admirer, Dr. Mann. Much more relaxed and secure, opened by friendship, Judith Sands actually shows Renate and Dr. Mann one of her manuscripts. Its opening words are the same words with which *Collages* begins!

This repetition helps to endow *Collages* with its circular structure at the same time that it underscores Anaïs Nin's conviction that art is the "alcheemical" magic through which life is redeemed. Our lives are ceaseless change, a never-ending process that moves from birth to maturity to decay and to the apparent death that is, in reality, a transformation of energy into a different form. Echoing the theme of the ragpickers' song are some wise words from the Koran that comfort the Consul's rejected wife: " 'Nothing is ever finished.' "[21] Once an interaction of two persons has begun, especially if it is a lively one, it cannot be stopped but will continue to affect both from then on, however subtly and indirectly.

The elements Nin uses in her prose collages are drawn without exception from her personal experience. They are the people, the relationships, the situations, and settings she actually knows. To these she adds the knowledge arising from her interpretations of unconscious dramas, dreams, visions, and intuitions. She emphasizes the validity of unconscious experience, which she carefully evokes and analyzes. The vast tissue of Nin's entwined life and writings reveals the fascinating way in which the self mediates between conscious and unconscious experience, traveling between them like an artful spider, building an intricate structure from the relationships it creates in its ceaseless motion. Thus Nin's sensibility may be observed at work with the materials of her experience, busily shaping feelings, intuitions, observations, and ideas into the personal relationships that are always her subject matter. The fixative in her collage compositions is always a self in relationship. And from the presence of this self radiate perceptions and insights that endow the collage, whether it is a volume of the diary or a novel, with its particular design of feeling and form. In the Diaries and the books of criticism, the self that controls the design is Nin's own; in the fiction the author's self is concealed behind projections of other selves, characters based upon women with whom the author identifies in some significant way. In every case, though, it is the motion of this self toward awareness that provides the stuff that holds together the other elements in the composition of the book. The glue in Nin's collages is the "I" who perceives, reflects, interacts with others, dreams, interprets her experience, and, finally, expresses what she has experienced.

The concept of the self is very important in any exploration of Nin's writings, and it is difficult to isolate a single definition of "self," notwithstanding the many references to it. Nin does not seem to be concerned with the self as essence. Instead, she writes about the self in motion, in relationships with others, learning, searching, suffering, recovering, gathering still more experience. In short, Nin writes about the self as a process, almost as an urge toward the discovery and completion of itself. Gradually, though, it seems that Nin has come close to adopting a basically Jungian idea of the self. This influence began with the period of psychoanalysis with Dr. Martha Jaeger and has received more emphasis in recent years because of Nin's friendship with Dr. Ira Progoff. It is particularly important to distinguish between the self and the *persona,* the mask or socialized dimension of a human being. Nin's fictional characters are often trying to discover their selves and to separate their authentic desires from the confusion caused by overly powerful *personae.* The glossary included in Jung's autobiography, *Memories, Dreams, Reflections,* defines self as "not only the centre but also the whole circumference which embraces both conscious and unconscious; it is the centre of this totality, just as the ego is the centre of the conscious mind."[22] In "The Writer and the Symbols," Nin defined the supreme aspiration of her work: "The quest of the self through the intricate maze of modern confusion is the central theme of my work. But you cannot reach unity and integration without patiently experiencing first of all the turns of the labyrinth of falsities and delusions in which man has lost himself. And you cannot transcend the personal by avoiding it, but by confronting it and coming to terms with it."[23]

These confrontations and self-discoveries provide the subject matter of Nin's novels, as of her Diaries. Besides dream interpretation and the revelations of free association, she has explored the ways in which a self is affected by the selves of those with whom it is deeply involved. In *The Novel of the Future,* she wrote: "We know now that *we are composites in reality,* collages of our fathers and mothers, of what we read, of television influences and films, of friends and associates . . ." Empowered by the act of perception, the self is a tool for connecting the conscious and unconscious realms. This is true of all people, but is much more obvious in the case of artists, whose completed work testifies to the success of the connections the self has accomplished. Since the self is individualized and each is unique, because of the varying elements of which each is composed, its way of seeing the world will necessarily be personal and, therefore, slightly different from that of any other individual. This is the source of the relativity to which Nin so often refers. Because each self has an individual vision, it is always in danger of distorting what it perceives. This is one more reason, in Nin's thought, why each individual needs to know his hidden self as deeply as possible, so as to discover his deficiencies in an attempt to correct his vision." The only objectivity we can reach is achieved, first of all, by an examination of our *self* as lens, as camera, as recorder, as mirror. Once we know its idiosyncrasies, its areas of prejudice or blindness, we can proceed to relate with others. We cannot relate to others without a self."[24]

In dramatizing the journey of an "I" toward recognition of its self, again and again Nin chooses to explore the complexity of relationships or the impact of two selves on each other. She uses the terms "fusion" and "merging" to describe intense personal relationships.[25] Her characters, like her own self in her Diary, are always moving either toward an experience of fusion or struggling to become free from one. Nin seems to agree with D. H. Lawrence that this vacillation is natural and necessary. At times the self requires a state of fusion, and will be disappointed and even thrown into despair when it fails to achieve it. But at other times the self requires privacy, an opportunity to experience its own nature in solitude without the obligation to fulfill the demands of the other. "A man who lives unrelated to other human beings dies. But a man who lives unrelated to himself also dies."[26] The self, then, is obliged to live with instability; it is committed to a life of motion between its own boundaries and the personal territories of other people's psyches. Yet it is through this continuous change and adjustment of its perceptions that the self comes to discover its own nature. Through knowing others, we come to know ourselves and eventually the world. ". . . I could identify with characters unlike myself, enter their vision of the universe, and *in essence* achieve the truest objectivity of all, *which is to be able to see what the other sees, to feel what the other feels.*"[27]

The discovery of self becomes possible in the process of living relationships, of constant interaction between the individual and phenomena, the individual and other people. "Life is a process of *becoming,* a combination of states we have to go through. Where people fail is that they wish to elect a state and remain in it. This is a kind of death."[28] Our perceptions of reality depend upon the experiences absorbed by the self, and the self we are at any moment in time is partly dependent upon the kinds of relationships of fusion we have experienced and the ways in which they have affected our identities. Nin's basic view of self and its unpredictable journey through experience was already a part of her thought when she wrote her book on Lawrence. As time passed and she learned more about psychology, this idea became more detailed and more sophisticated, but her essential insight into the nature of fusion, the way in which one person seeks to fuse with another, was originally intuitive.

There are several possible motivations for the attempt to fuse one's identity with that of another person or persons. One of the most obvious is a sense of incompleteness or fragmentation. Fusion may complement one's sense of identity, as in intense friendship or romantic love; the partners may be of the same or of opposite sexes. Merging, when it implies the submersion of a weaker in a stronger person's sense of identity, may have its origin in the same desire for a stronger sense of self but actually lead to a weakening of this identity when the personality of the stronger absorbs that of the more dependent person. These are negative examples of fusion or of merging. In Nin's early writing the dangers do, in fact, outweigh the psychic advantages of such close relationship. As Nin moves into maturity, however, this anxiety gradually begins to disappear. The fear of fragmentation and loss of autonomy is slowly replaced

by a confident reaching outward to enhance the self through a
variety of identifications and intimate associations. Nin's early prose
works explore the terror of loss of self, either because of fear and
inhibition, or because of a dependency that a weak person has disguised as infatuation or love. Paralysis of feeling, numbness, inability to experience emotion, as well as hypersensitivity, an uncon-
trolled capacity for empathy, can cause the self to split into
seemingly unrelated parts. Variations on this theme are portrayed
in *House of Incest,* in some of the stories printed in *Under a Glass
Bell,* in "Stella" and "Winter of Artifice," and in *Ladders to Fire.*

House of Incest, Nin's earliest published "fiction," is an imagistic
enactment in poetic prose of a woman's "perilous" journey. The "I"
desperately longs to expand the dimensions of herself through
fusion with two other women who dominate her dreams with re-
lentless constancy and force.

Inspired by Rimbaud's *Une Saison en Enfer, House of Incest*
portrays the psychic torment of a woman who can experience love
but not her physical nature. She cannot express sensuality or sexuality. The language of Nin's book evokes an oppressive atmosphere
of erotic tantalization and paralysis; impossible pleasures beckon
from every direction. The unnamed "I" is the center of the design.
Her alternating yearnings to lose herself in one or the other of the
book's phantom women give the composition its tension, the inter-
play of the "I" among her obsessive fantasies of Sabina and Jeanne,
both of whom represent an unhealthy but intense relationship to
eroticism. Inhibited, hypersensitive, paralyzed by neurotic conflict,
the "I" is strongly attracted to the forms of fascination represented
by these contrasting figures: toward the spontaneous, unthinking
acting upon any sensuous desire, on the one hand; on the other,
toward the alluring, forbidden, intense love of the brother, toward
a sterile but safe love. In order to resist both modes of identification
and resolution, the one infantile, the other perverse, the "I" must
embark upon a journey into the House of Incest.

Like the "I" of *House of Incest,* the young woman at the center
of "Winter of Artifice" seeks to expand her identity through an act
of psychic fusion. The novella is a collage of relatively homogene-

ous elements that are held into design by the consciousness of the dominant—again unnamed—central personage. Again, too, a psychic adventure with fusion has a strong individual tone which gives the book its appropriate metaphors and rhythms. Projecting the love of daughter and father, Nin in "Winter of Artifice" evokes and interprets the ambivalence of fusion that she described in her book on Lawrence, defending this ambivalence as an essential factor in all relationships of deep involvement.

Again the reader is shown that fusion, though necessary to the ego of the developing self, poses serious risks to identity. One may be unwise in the choice of partner and find oneself lost, submerged, consumed by the other. This danger is the greater if it is a parent with whom one seeks to merge. The parent is usually stronger, and moreover is endowed with a seductive accumulation of experience, an air of authority and wisdom that feed the child's fantasy of being able to obtain anything, to heal any wound, by appealing to the all-powerful parent. Because of his original biological dependence, a child may easily lose his sense of self in the relationship with the mother. But the relationship with the father also presents a threat, particularly to the daughter Nin portrays; she suffers doubly from the expectations and needs of a child and those of a fantasizing lover. The daughter's yearning for fusion is intensified, as Nin explores this conflict in "Winter of Artifice," because of the twenty-year period during which she has been separated from her father. The daughter feels an almost irresistible pressure to hurl herself emotionally into the past to recapture this lost time. Gradually though, through intelligent analysis of her father's character, Nin's heroine is able to withstand the threat to her psychic autonomy. Her "womanly" way of conquering her vain father is to offer him an irresistible form of mothering. In an effort to avoid giving his love, the father cleverly chooses to regard his daughter as an "Amazon." Amazons, of course, do not need men. As long as the daughter collaborates in this perception of herself, she permits her father to continue to refuse all responsibility for her needs and desires.

Finally, the daughter confronts the reality of her father's selfishness. She strips away his "mask" (a frequent image) to disclose the manipulative and childish person beneath the elegant facade. "It was a struggle with shadows [when Jeanne kisses her brother in *House of Incest,* she is said to kiss a "shadow"] . . . . No one had ever merged with her father, yet they had thought a fusion could be realized through the likeness between them but the likeness itself seemed to create greater separations and confusions. There was a likeness and no understanding, likeness and no nearness."[29] In "Winter of Artifice" the desire for fusion is intense and even exciting, but it fails because of the threat it poses to the daughter's sense of identity, to her desire for personal liberty.

As she has repeatedly told her readers, Anaïs Nin's most valuable resource as an artist is her own complex self. Picking and choosing from the many and varied experiences of this self, she has created her ingenious books by combining elements that would not be found together in traditional fiction. She welds odds and ends of experience into collage compositions with the intensity of her personal vision of self and reality. As she has grown and changed, so have her books, reflecting the life that gave rise to them, just as the life has fed upon and been nourished by the books.

The quest that is traced again and again in Nin's writings actually involves a very radical concept: the abandonment of the idea of the self as a given fixed entity or essence. We create ourselves as we live, Nin explains poetically in her books and in the example of her own life that is revealed in the Diary. The idea of the self as a collage of experiences is central to Nin's psychological vision. Max Ernst, in writing of collage, quotes André Breton: " 'Who knows if we are not somehow preparing ourselves to escape from the principle of identity?' "[30]

Such a question naturally provokes another: "escape" into *what*? Nin would no doubt share Breton's enthusiasm for escaping from the old-fashioned idea of identity as something fixed and given for all time, and she would welcome this escape as freeing people to meet the psychological challenges of the age of relativity, challenges which, from quite another perspective, were anticipated by Henri Bergson when he wrote *Creative Evolution.* The self is always engaged in the process of change, always modifying itself, altering, adapting, searching, expanding, growing ever closer to its most complete expression. Once again, relationship is the key to Nin's view of the self as a relativistic entity. "What happens is that two people [or three, or more] create a new alchemy. They interact upon each other and what takes place is not the leadership of one over the other, but the consequences of this interaction."[31] There are no limits to the powers of expansion of the self, not if the center is fortified. However, if the center has neither been accepted nor developed (and this is the case, for example, with Stella and Sabina), there is danger of fragmentation, disintegration, and destruction. Nin stresses the crucial difference between fragmentation and multiplicity: "rich personalities have many aspects but do not fall apart."[32] In 1961 Nin was able to write with confidence: "The 'self' in my work is merely an instrument of awareness, the center of consciousness and experience, but it is like the self in Proust, a mirror for many other personalities, it is the core from which spring all kinds of relationships to others . . . . There is a constant, an organic preoccupation with development and growth."[33]

In Nin's life and art alike increasing complexity and increasing clarity have grown together as the self has passed from one experience and one relationship to another, always searching for meaning. Nin's desire for understanding has been enhanced by her artist's desire to "animate" knowledge, to give it the vitality and the unpredictability of life. "Relating one thing to another is almost what I would call a form of spontaneous life. The fusion of them is the alchemist's brew. I prefer my knowledge animated—that is, represented by a human being: a great doctor, an architect, or a painter. The living arts and humanities, caught in the moment of creating, talking, living."[34]

Symphonic Writing

We write, like Proust, to render all of it eternal, and to per-
suade ourselves that it is eternal. We write to be able to transcend our life, to reach beyond it. We write to teach ourselves
to speak with others, to record the journey into the labyrinth,
we write to expand our world when we feel strangled, con-
stricted, lonely. We write as the birds sing. As the primitive
dance their rituals. If you do not breathe through writing, then
don't write.

—Diary of Anaïs Nin, Volume V

In the first published volume of her Diary, Anaïs Nin has described her childhood in a home where both mother and father were
artists who created around their children "an atmosphere of music
and books." The little girl was "always constructing, creating, writing, drawing, inventing plays, acting in them, writing a diary, living
in created dreams as inside a cocoon."[1] It was natural that Nin
grew up admiring the artist. Her father knew the flamboyant poet,
D'Annunzio. The Nin household was filled with the aura of the later
Symbolists at the turn of the century: Wilde, Valéry, Debussy,
Fauré. Their ideas about art have had a decisive and lasting influence on Anaïs Nin, though like all original people, she has greatly
transformed the influences she has absorbed in the process of adapting them to the expressive needs of her own temperament.

Like the Symbolists, Nin believes that phenomena possess hidden
meanings, significances that escape the average person. The artist's
task is to penetrate surfaces to reveal the truths they conceal. "The
symbol," she has written, "is an acknowledgement of the emotional
and spiritual content of every act and every object around us."
Equipped with heightened perception and expressive talent, the
artist can interpret this vast confusing world of phenomena—veri-

19

fiable reality—giving us the revelations of essences that we need to feel at ease in a world of masks and disguises. Nin has described a story as "a quest for meaning."[2] A character, a situation, a place, even a title or a phrase, may fascinate a writer. He may then, in the process of accepting the challenge of solving a mystery, create for us a work of art.

With the Symbolists, too, Nin shares a positive attitude toward dream and fantasy. Her writing is a poetic defense of her belief in the unconscious as a source of the visions and imaginary experiences that complement life, compensating for its limitations, endowing it with the richness of mental play and the dreamed-of fulfillments that "reality" may not be capable of providing. In *Collages* Nin goes further than merely defending fantasy, she actually celebrates it as a source of magic much needed by those who live bare and sometimes despairing lives. This deliberate rejection of the outer in favor of the inner life was the "decadence" of the Symbolists; in Nin's work it is an early tendency that has undergone an evolution as her ideas and her art have matured. Nin stresses the positive aspects of fantasy in order to balance American society's mistrust, fear, and even condemnation of mental activities that are not directly productive in a materialist way.[3]

A deep, an especially important love of the Symbolists which Nin shares is music, a love so powerful that it inspired the efforts of poets like Verlaine and Mallarmé to transform poetry into music: Verlaine with liquid harmonies of sound and Mallarmé with structures that were designed to approximate the intricacy of musical forms. All her life Nin has sought to musicalize her writing. Finally, Nin shares the Symbolists' elevation of the artist to an almost religious significance (though this, admittedly, is characteristic of much modernist thought). It was Rimbaud who tried to restore status and dignity to the artist by proclaiming the poet a *voyant,* or seer, a modern-day magician.[4] Nin has explained: "In every form of art there is something that I wanted to include, and I wanted writing, poetic writing, to include them all. Because I thought always of art not only as a balm, as a consolation, but I thought of art, as I said, as a supreme act of magic."[5] The artist is one who makes visible the invisible, and in Anaïs Nin's view the invisible is essential as the complement of the visible. The more society stresses a materialist interpretation of reality, the more necessary are artists who possess the capacity to objectify the unseen, or unverifiable, dimensions of reality. This is a tenet of modernism that goes back to Romanticism, later finding powerful restatement by Apollinaire, Kandinsky, Max Ernst, André Breton, and many other thinkers who have deplored the biases and dangers of an exaggerated emphasis on the empirical approach to and interpretation of experience.[6]

Along with Proust, whose influence on *Cities of the Interior* is great and whose influence on Nin's Diary is even greater, Janko Varda is one of the artists most admired by Nin. In "The Poetic Reality of Anaïs Nin," Anna Balakian remarks how Varda in Nin's later work replaces the father figures (Miller, Allendy, Rank) of the earlier work.[7] Varda might be called Nin's spiritual father. His robust life, enjoyed fully to the final moment, and his shimmering, delicate, inventive collage art alike inspired her exuberant praise. In July 1952, she wrote in her Diary how she experienced the sensation of actually stepping into or becoming part of a collage Varda had given her and which hung in her apartment. This strange visionary experience followed several irritating events capped by "a visit from drunken friends." "I fixed my eyes on the Varda collage. It was as if I had stepped out of my life into a region of sand composed of crystals, of transparent women dancing in airy dresses, figures which no obstacle could stop, who could pass through walls, beings designed like sieves to allow the breeze through. Through these floating figures with openings like windows, life could flow." The delicious freedom she felt upon imagining herself a part of the collage released her from the torment of thinking of herself as "a caged animal." Somewhat comforted but sorrowful, Nin concludes that Varda succeeded in attaining the state of total freedom that she longs for. "Varda reached freedom and I did not, but only because his image, being visible to the human eye, was stronger than the moments I describe and enclose in a book."[8]

Nin's literary aspiration is formidable; it is to express passionately and powerfully what others are not aware of, or if they are, cannot express because they do not possess the means of articulation. This aspiration poses a special problem, a frustration, for it is easy to describe what everyone has seen or has experienced with his own senses, but it is a far greater challenge to choose words that are vital with the power to render the invisible or the unknown in a way that is vivid and sensuous. Nin has been searching for "another kind of language, the inspirational, which is the one that *penetrates our unconscious directly* [italics mine] and doesn't need to be analyzed or interpreted in a cerebral way. It penetrates us in the way that music does, through the senses."[9] In denoting or pointing to objects and even to concepts, the word is more precise than the musical note or phrase, but verbal expression is more abstract, less direct in sensuous power than are the sounds, colors, forms, and rhythms of the nonverbal arts. That is why Nin, like so many other twentieth-century writers, has borrowed as widely as possible from the other arts. "My only structure," she writes, "is based on three forms of art — painting, dancing, music—because they correspond to the senses I find atrophied in literature today."[10] Even as late as the 1950s when Nin had attained a fairly strong sense of identity as a creator, she still suffered from the sense that her writing lacked the expressive freedom and power that she found in Varda's collages and in Proust's descriptive prose: "I immerse myself in his [Proust's] world. He is more alive through his senses, his passion for every detail of his life, than a thousand so-called realists, because it is passion which recreates a flower, a leaf, a cathedral spire, a sunset, a meal. And how he struggles to give each object its meaning."[11]

Inspired by many artists including Debussy, Paul Klee, Varda, of course; Richard Lippold, Jean Tinguely, Edgar Varèse and her good friend the painter Frances Field, Nin looked not so much to poets for her models (though Rimbaud has influenced her style as well as her ideas) as to those novelists who were masters of a lyrical yet analytical style: to Lawrence, Giraudoux, Pierre Jean Jouve, Djuna Barnes, and, above all, to Proust. Nin's approach to the novel is that of a poet with a heightened and highly developed sense of language.[12] The image is her indispensable medium of expression, and the abandonment to free association is the process through which organic structures emerge for her. Nin's subject is the self in the evolution toward growth and toward freedom, the self in relationships. Her perspective is always psychological (she calls psychology her "philosophy"), her perceptions always profound. She cannot be accused of presenting demonstrations of any particular school of psychological interpretation.

Dispensing with plot and with the framework of conventional chronology, Nin portrays her characters again and again in a series of "shots" that depend for their power on the imagery of highly selective detail. Her language is metaphorical but never purely decorative. It is the language of lyrical poetry through which a personal attitude is compressed in a few words or phrases that express an individual sensibility. Nin does not describe. She interprets, and in the act of interpretation she re-creates her subjects over and over again, as she must do if she is to be faithful to their complexity and their growth. To know Nin's characters the reader, too, must interpret their actions and thoughts. He must interpret the patterns that give meaning to the lives of these characters. Free association, of course, creates its own structures. Nin's writing is filled with patterns that are natural and spontaneous, having emerged from associations. The form is organic; it consists of repetitions; inversions; superimpositions; and, more and more often in Nin's later prose, of improvisatory flights in which images are often treated as are themes in jazz. Fluency, fluidity, a sense of motion, and of continuity are what Nin seeks in her writing, an orchestration of a great many elements into a composition that moves through time horizontally and vertically at the same instant, expressing emotion with a power that is impossible to attain in conventional realistic fiction.

Nin's early books *House of Incest* and *Under a Glass Bell* delight readers who can yield to the intoxication of language. The former is a dream piece; literally, it consists of edited and polished dreams. A "prose poem," *House of Incest* is comprised entirely of images; consequently, it has a feverish, hallucinatory quality. Nin has never again devoted herself totally to the image as her exclusive mode of verbal expression.[13] The collection *Under a Glass Bell,* which brought Nin her first critical attention in the U.S., contains the essential themes of her major work and the larger controlling metaphors that recur in her later books. The pieces brought together in *Bell* were written between 1935 and 1942 or 1943. They are called "stories," but only "The Mouse" tells a story, and even this one is more like a sketch or personal memoir than a conventional short story. Nin does not develop situations around her characters, bringing them to a dramatic climax before providing a resolution, either through action or revelation and acceptance of some important truth by the central figures. Usually, there are no crises and resolutions. The pieces in *Under a Glass Bell* are imagistically rendered presentations of persons or of conflicts. Nin makes no attempt at development of her materials. Her purpose is to portray persons and situations in depth, caught for an instant in revealing postures or attitudes. Nin probes for these postures and attitudes and casts them up in brilliant and sometimes strange metaphors.

The atmosphere of *Under a Glass Bell* is much like that of *House of Incest,* oppressive, stale, dusty, hard, chalky. As the title indicates, the recurrent situation expresses frustration, despair, loss, or paralysis. City officials of Paris send a houseboat into exile, banishing it from the bustling center of the city. Jeanne is here, as well as in *House of Incest,* envisioning herself in her tomb. The Mohican, a scholar of the occult, is jailed by the Germans when they invade Paris. Pierre, a thin disguise for Antonin Artaud, is confined to a mental asylum. Hopelessly seeking his twin in love, Jean is trapped behind the windows of his apartment which he has painted closed so as to shut out the life beyond. Like Pierre, the painter in "The Eye's Journey" is imprisoned by a self-destructive fear; he too, must go to an asylum. A child with a black father and white mother is condemned to social exile in "The Child Born Out of the Fog." Hedja, in the sketch of the same name, frees herself from her native Persia, a country of veils and harems, to pass through subsequent forms of veiling that are equally oppressive. In "The Mouse" and "Birth" conceptions do not develop into new lives. Instead, the potential mothers must endure physical suffering only to lose the infants they might have borne and, under different circumstances, have nurtured and loved.

Here in *Bell* are two of the main themes of Nin's later work: woman's conflicts (particularly with the role of mother) and the struggle of the artist to achieve joyous, unrestrained power of expression. The metaphors that Nin introduces in this collection appear again and again in her later work. She uses them not only to bind together her impressions in a single sketch but also to weave a unifying strand through the book. The image of the title is perfect as a description of the psychic states of all the book's figures: imprisonment in a small, airless enclosure, an imprisonment of the psyche. The walls of the prison are transparent, but they are also impassable. The persons trapped under the bell can see outside into the world beyond, but they cannot break through the glass to live in that world. Nin writes of the tragedy of awareness when it is unsupported by creative will.

In *Under a Glass Bell,* everything that should move or be used is paralyzed. The houseboat is retired to a mooring outside the center of activity. Jeanne's guitar string breaks. Her brother Jean's guitar is nailed to the wall but never used. Pierre (Artaud) is terrified of descending into the abyss of his madness. At the end of "Je Suis le Plus Malade des Surrealistes" the madman falls on his face because his feet have been bound by the doctor and his aides. Hans, a painter, is like Pierre; he, too, has descended to "a shipwreck of broken moods, lost fragments of irretrievable worlds."[14] "The Labyrinth" and "Through the Streets of My Own Labyrinth" express Nin's fear (a temporary one) that her diary was an obsessive activity that was preventing her from directing her energy toward other more public forms of writing, a mindless motion without direction "between the walls and fortresses of [her] diary."[15] Finally, the most disturbing failure of movement to be meaningful is in "Birth." The woman labors to expel the child from her womb. But the baby is already dead.

The images of these early pieces appear again and again in Nin's fiction and in her Diaries: water, boats, musical instruments, mirrors, labyrinths, veils, shadows and fogs, blood, birds, voyages, dreams, births. But each image has an individual history of variations in presentation, diversity, and complexity, as Nin explores each one in a variety of moods and at various periods in her own development. As Nin herself evolved, acquiring confidence and energy as a writer, the artists who were trapped by addictions, by madness or stubborn neurosis gradually disappear from her work. The painter Hans was unable to use the junk he had collected: "All that could fall from a ragpicker's bag lay heaving restlessly buried by Hans . . ."[16] This failure is overcome by the gaiety and energetic will of Varda, while the childish Hedja, whose paintings grow larger and brighter as she rediscovers her primitivism, is replaced by the sculptor Cornelia Runyon, who appears in *Diary V* along with Renate, the mature central figure of *Collages*.[17]

"Winter of Artifice," begun in 1933 and completed in 1939, is a mature work, very sophisticated technically, in which Anaïs Nin first fully displays her talent for adapting the structure of the non-verbal arts to fiction. It is a ballet of words in which music and movement are so skillfully balanced and so subtly interwoven that, though the perceptive reader may be always aware of a musical quality as he reads, he isn't likely to be distracted by the search to identify the predominating musical medium. The novella's sixty-four pages are organized in thirteen movements of unequal length. As is usual in Nin's writing, there is no mention of chronology. It is not the passage of time, the sequence of events, but the personalized patterns that bestow meaning on characters and situations.

The theme is of "Musique Ancienne," a variation on the Oedipal drama.[18] At the beginning of the novella a daughter, who is un-named, awaits a visit from her father. Memories fill in details of the past and their separation during her childhood. In the third movement the father arrives, initiating an intense interval, a symbolic *lune de miel* between daughter and father. They travel to the south of France. There they tease themselves, inflaming ardor by pretend-ing to be engaged. To the daughter her father represents an idealized lover, an all-powerful father, and—finally—a god. To the father, the daughter is, however, just another woman to be conquered, subdued by his charm, and attached to him in submission to his needs. She is a potential ornament for his salon. The narrative mingles the daughter's memories and observations with passages of dialogue; thus the motion in time is forward and backward simultaneously. The novella attains a climax of emotional and erotic fantasy in the sixth, or center, passage. Here the daughter allows herself to *imagine* union with her father. This is conveyed in strongly cadenced, sensuous prose:

> Inside both their heads, as they sat there, he leaning against a pillow and she against the foot of the bed, there was a concert going on. Two boxes filled with the resonances of an orchestra. A hundred instruments playing all at once. Two long spools of flutethreads interweaving between his past and hers, the strings of the violin constantly trembling like the strings inside their bodies, the nerves never still, the heavy poundings on the drum like the heavy pounding of sex, the throb of blood, the beat of desire which drowned all the vibrations, louder than any instrument. . . .

This rhapsody is extended and brilliantly sustained to conclude with the question, more a plea than a question: *"Can we live in rhythm, my father? Can we feel in rhythm, my father? Can we think in rhythm, my father? Rhythm—rhythm—rhythm."*[19]

From this peak, the work subsides into a slower rhythm, a sadder tone. The flirtation of the two has been expressed as a long, complex, formal dance in which they have moved toward each other and away again, sometimes moving together, sometimes separately, but always circling, always attracted but wary, tentative, frightened.

But after the crisis of the fantasized union, the dance becomes a solo for the daughter who moves away from her father. This is portrayed through a series of metaphors and one important incident involving dance. In the seventh movement they are once again in Paris, and the daughter recalls having given a performance when she was sixteen at which she imagined having seen her proud and approving father in the audience. When she asks him about this, he denies having been there. "He answered that not only was he not there but that if he had had the power he would have prevented her from dancing because he did not want his daughter on the stage."[20] A snob, rigid and old-fashioned, this father wants his daughter to be a "lady." He wants to imprison her with senseless restrictions.

As soon as she makes this discovery the daughter begins to be able to free herself. Upon seeing her father's "feminine-looking" foot, she imagines that it is really her foot and has been stolen from her by her father. Indeed, now she understands that he would like to appropriate her mobility for himself. But the father suffers, appropriately, from lumbago. "Tired of his ballet dancing" (a formal, traditional, externally patterned dance), the daughter symbolically reclaims her foot and, with it her ability to flee. *"Music runs and I run with it. Faith makes music come out of the trees, out of wood, out of ivory."*[21]

The beauty and strength of feet, suggesting not only the artful motion of dance, but also the power of flight, is a recurrent metaphor in Nin's writing. Stella moves with "a lightness which belongs to other races, the race of ballet dancers." Like Djuna, she adores beautiful shoes. In "The Voice" Djuna's mobility is praised by Lilith, who suffers from a paralyzing frigidity: "You say everything with your body, like a dancer. All your body talks, your hands, your walk." One of The Voice's patients fears that she is a Lesbian, but the doctor does not agree: "He felt the woman in her through her feet, through her hands. They transmitted a woman current."[22] "By touching [Sabina's] naked foot, [Donald] had felt a unity with the mother, early memories of an existence within the silk, warmth and effortlessness of a vast love."[23] It is fitting that Sabina usually wears sandals. Nin often suggests the paralysis of neurosis or deep fear of life, by some sort of crippling. In her Diaries, where she so often expresses the pleasure and release of dancing, Nin records her disappointment that Otto Rank had to be coaxed to dance.[24] Jeanne of *House of Incest* has a crippled leg, as does a minor character in "The Voice," Mischa.

In Nin's work, dance symbolizes not only freedom and independence but also, on occasion, an interesting form of defiance. Such is the erotic dance of Sabina and Lillian in *Ladders to Fire,* which antagonizes the men in a French tavern. There are several dance scenes in *Seduction of the Minotaur:* Lillian deliberately uses dance to express her criticism of one man, her approval of others. When Michael Lomax takes her to his home among the ruins, a group of Mexican students arrive in a joyous, spontaneous mood to create a street festival. Michael tries to thwart Lillian's pleasure by warning her that the students " 'like to be alone, among men.' "[25] Ignoring his objections, she dances in the street with the students, the only woman among them, happily receiving their compliments and serenades. The inference is that Michael wants to limit not only Lillian's gaiety, but also her sexuality. She defies his prudery.

The three central figures of *Cities* can be associated with characteristic individual dance movements: Djuna's is an airy flight, a whirl through space, light and graceful; Sabina's is heavier, an erotic dance of fire best performed in one of the nightclubs she frequently haunts; Lillian's is simple, an earthy peasant dance done with bare feet slapping the soil. Djuna, however, is a dancer by profession, and the novel that is most deeply imbued with the spirit of dance is one in which she is featured, *Children of the Albatross*. Djuna's painful childhood as an orphan is compared to "heavy walking on crutches," but when she learned to dance, this young woman "discovered the air, space and the lightness of her own nature." In life Djuna feels split and fragmented, "but at the moment of dancing a fusion took place, a welding, a wholeness. The cut in the middle of her body healed, and she was all one woman moving." Djuna's self-confidence and her strength develop because of the flattering attention of her former dancing master.

But the Djuna of *Children* is not yet ready for a committed love. She has playful friendships with several "children" ("airy young men"). Although dancing is associated with flight, with movement, with living, it is also connected with erotic play and with the act of healing, which entails belief. "Dancing and believing." The enthusiastic Lawrence "accepted every invitation. His joy was in movement, in assenting, in consenting, in expansion. Whenever he came he lured Djuna into a swirl. Even in sadness they smiled at each other, expanding in sadness with dilated eyes and dilated hearts. 'Drop every sorrow and dance!' Thus they healed each other by dancing, perfectly mated in enthusiasm and fire."

Her disappointing relationship with Michael is one of the sorrows Djuna strives to heal. The passage that describes their relationship is worth quoting in its entirety; it is a fine example of how Nin's imagery embodies and expands upon theme:

> Because of their youth and their moving still outside of the center of their own desires blindly, what they danced together was not a dance in which either took possession of the other, but a kind of minuet, where the aim consisted in *not* appropriating, *not* grasping, *not* touching, but allowing the maximum space and distance to flow between the two figures. To move in accord without collisions, without merging. To encircle, to bow in worship, to laugh at the same absurdities, to mock their own movements, to throw upon the walls twin shadows which will never become one. To dance around this danger: the danger of becoming one! To dance keeping each to his own path. To allow parallelism, but no loss of the self into the other. To play at marriage, step by step, to read the same book together, to dance a dance of elusiveness on the rim of desire, to remain within circles of heightened lighting without touching the core that would set the circle on fire.

> A deft dance of unpossession.

Michael may be the same man who, in *Seduction of the Minotaur,* tries to prevent Lillian from joining in the festival, or from dancing with other men; it is jealousy, in fact, which destroys Djuna and the younger Michael's potential for relationship, for fusion, for becoming one in the emotional and physical act of love. Djuna's enjoyment of dancing with others besides himself infuriates and alienates Michael. *Children of the Albatross* is not, however, focused on Djuna's relationships with Lawrence or Michael, but on her love affair with Paul. When he departs for India, Djuna, who also longs to travel, feels abandoned and sad. Just as she had done as a child when she hid herself under a large shawl and pretended to be "traveling," Djuna turns to fantasy for consolation. She allows herself to dream, inspired by her collection of shoes from all over the world. And she dances. For the time being, Djuna's dance is a "ballet of oscillations,"[26] for she, like Paul, is attracted to but not yet prepared for the intense dance of fusion in which two become one.

Dance unites several of Nin's most important themes: the power of art, which is itself its own goal; the possibility of turning to beauty for therapy and for healing; the association of movement and pattern with the life process. It is essential not simply to move but to move to a meaningful rhythm. In all of Nin's writing there is no figure of dance that surpasses the beauty of the image which closes *House of Incest.* The woman who was punished for clinging to her loves learns to accept and to relinquish. She learns the necessity of fusion and of separation. She learns to hear celestial music; her dance is reminiscent of the cosmic dance of the god Shiva: "And she danced; she danced with the music and with the rhythm of earth's circles; she turned with the earth turning, like a disk, turning all faces to light and to darkness evenly, dancing towards daylight."[27]

Besides providing an important metaphor, dance has given Nin a model of structure. She has recorded how, writing the party scene in *Ladders to Fire,* she used choreographic patterns borrowed from the work of Martha Graham. "I fused symbols and externals." Nin adds, "My greatest inspiration comes from the work of other artists: the subtle, suggestive, mysterious world of Martha Graham; the modern painters; modern music . . ."[28] Nin often imitates dance structure in alternating solos or duets with large group scenes. Parties and café ensembles occur throughout the novels of *Cities of the Interior* like rituals, bringing disparate elements into moments of splendid unity, moments of celebration. Sometimes Nin includes in these scenes characters who never again appear. In *The Four-Chambered Heart,* a Paris street fair is the means of revealing Djuna's lonely childhood and her love of dance. In three of the five novels, the characters come together in a café. These scenes sparkle with friendly discussions of art and gossip. They evoke the ambiance of Paris in the 1930s. The communal scenes of *A Spy in the House of Love,* set in the United States, appropriately take place in night clubs. *Seduction of the Minotaur* and *Collages* also contain vivid gatherings in places of entertainment or hotels.

The practice of alternating group scenes with more solitary or intimate ones gives a structure of alternating rhythms and moods. Thematically, this alternation stresses the subjective and objective worlds that Anaïs Nin constantly strives to bring together into moments of fusion. The café or party scenes usually come near the end of a novel. Just when the reader expects something predictable to happen to a certain character, this individual is swept off the stage into the wings, to be replaced by a chorus, by new forms, by new voices. This suggests an expansion of possibilities for the solo dancer. Anaïs Nin ends each novel by reminding her characters— and readers—of new worlds. Instead of closing down with a neat, rounded-off (classical) resolution, she makes her novels open up at the end, exploding into a variety of surprising directions. Nin herself approved of the effect she achieved in *Ladders to Fire:* "I like the party section. It is like one of Martha Graham's ballets; it was inspired by them. It is full of rhythm and color. It is like a mobile, a modern painting."[29]

The rhythm and color that Nin infuses into her writing often arise from passages devoted to paintings. A film, "the story of the Atlantis accompanied by the music of Stravinski," shocks Stella, thrusting her toward a deeper knowledge of herself. The first scene is "like a Paul Klee, wavering and humid, delicate and full of vibrations."[30] As Stella yields to these images, she senses a floating, dissolving, motion, a relaxed state of mind in which she is able to explore the series of personal shocks that have, in the past, interfered with her maturity. The language of images penetrates our rationally constructed defenses; art speaks to us directly. Art educates the emotions.

Nin sometimes uses paintings to reveal character. They become metaphors for personality traits, yielding their revelations through associations. When Lillian visits the silent, windless ruins of the city where Michael Lomax lives, she is reminded of Giorgio di Chirico's metaphysical paintings; this confirms her intuition of Michael's elusive and indirect nature. He is like a mysterious landscape in which no one moves. The sort of mutual dependence that stifles individuality is represented by Picasso's painting of two

figures tied to one breathing tube. The most brilliant use of painting in Nin's fiction counterpoints two contrasting images of Sabina.
Near the end of *A Spy in the House of Love* she meets her former
lover Jay. He has painted her as "a mandrake with fleshly roots,
bearing a solitary purple flower in a purple-bell-shaped corolla of
narcotic flesh."[31] Sabina is disturbed by this painting. Jay has interpreted her according to his own need; this one-dimensional view
from a limited perspective results in a fragment, a small part of the
truth masquerading as a portrait. Since there is much more to her
nature than exotic sexuality, Sabina must search for a more authentic image of herself. She discovers this in Duchamp's famous painting, "Nude Descending a Staircase."

But this discovery is not comforting. Although Jay's concept
was simplistic, Sabina's recognition of herself in the "Nude" is
equally disturbing because it exposes her emptiness: "Eight or ten
outlines of the same woman, like many multiple exposures of a
woman's personality, neatly divided into many layers, walking down
the stairs in unison."[32] Sabina is complex, but she lacks substance,
a center to give unity and clarity to her divided selves. In the contrast between these two approaches to painting, Nin alludes to the
unsatisfying distortions of the single point of view in art. Jay has not
considered the validity of any perspective on Sabina's nature except his own. He has captured the only part of her nature to which
he can feel related. He has left out everything else. Duchamp, a key
figure in modern art, recognizes the complexity not only of the
artist's perspective but also of the subject, of life itself, of being;
his representation of woman is closer to truth and, therefore, more
genuinely "realistic."

Jay's painting is, in fact, destructive. He makes "caricatures,"
Sabina accuses, adding, "He exposes only the ugly." The way in
which Jay paints, as well as his paintings, reveal his inner life, what
Nin calls his own "particular jungle." "In his very manner of press-
ing the paint tube there was intensity; often it spurted like a geyser,
was wasted, stained his clothes and the floor. The paint, having appeared in a minor explosion, proceeded to cause a major one on
the canvas. The explosions caused not a whole world to appear, but

a shattered world of fragments. Bodies, objects, cities, trees, animals were all splintered, pierced, impaled. It was actually a spectacle of carnage."[33] Compare Jay's art of dissociated fragments, which is admittedly powerful, to the collage composition of Varda. Jay splinters his subjects, but Varda gathers up fragments and arranges them into a new whole, fusing the pieces with his intelligence and sensitivity.

On one of the most dazzling pages of *Cities of the Interior,* which contains so many examples of sensuous writing, Nin blends references to painting and to music in a superb description of Mexican sunlight: "Just as music was an unbroken chain in Golconda, so were the synchronizations of color."[34] In *Seduction of the Minotaur* gold predominates; it is the symbol of illumination, the goal, in alchemy of a four-stage process signified by four colors: black; white; red; and, finally, the gold itself. Lillian plays jazz piano at the Black Pearl, a name whose symbolism unites seeming paradoxes. Golconda is the place of transformation for Lillian, the place where she "turns and changes," emerging from the labyrinth of her personal past to be borne away to a new life as her airplane carries her back to the U.S. The analogy between psychological discovery and alchemy is clear; the next to the last stage in the alchemical process is representative of dedication to spiritual striving and is often rendered in emblematic designs by a wingless creature being carried aloft by a winged being. "Alchemy may be seen as the pattern of all other work."[35] Its goal is the transformation that gradually creates a state of supreme illumination envisioned as golden. Iridescence, luminescence, radiance, all possess great importance in the symbolism of Nin's writing, for they indicate the capacity for transparency (openness, the stripping away of veils), for fluidity and mobility. Things that sparkle and shine have a positive value in Nin's writing, and when they are gold the heat of fire is also suggested, endowing the object or situation with vital energy and solar fire.

The Four-Chambered Heart shows Nin's skill in associating certain colors with character, situation, and theme. A constant contrast to the novel's aura of dampness, the frequent grey atmosphere, is the red lantern which Rango and Djuna use to welcome each other aboard their barge, and which they keep lighted when they are making love. As everyone knows, red is associated with sensuality, sexuality, and passion. Naturally, it is Sabina's color: "All dressed in red and silver, the tearing red and silver siren cutting a pathway through the flesh. The first time one looked at Sabina, one felt: everything will burn!" The volcanic Rango is associated with earth colors which contain a lot of red. He has "warm sienna" skin and the pupils of his eyes are "charcoal-colored." The passage which opens *The Four-Chambered Heart* is a near-repetition of the one which is used to introduce Rango at the party which brings *Ladders to Fire* to a close. Now Rango's skin tone has become "copper." Rango names the lantern he and Djuna use on their barge the "aphrodisiac lamp," but there is an early prophecy of destruction when he breaks the chimney while making love to her:" "the red glass broke, the oil burst into many small wild flames. She watched it without fear. Fire delighted her, and she had always wanted to live near danger." The drunken watchman who harasses the lovers insults Djuna and enrages Rango with his song which includes the lines, "Nanette gives love/Under a red lantern." Nonetheless, Rango continues to light the lantern "for her arrival, for her to see the red light from afar, to be reassured, incited to walk faster, elated by this symbol of his presence and his fervor."

Later, when Rango gives in to his former habits of laziness and inertia, Djuna lights the lantern for him. She even buys a small barrel of red wine which she places at the head of the bed, for she had faith that "their warmth together would take the place of the warmth of the wine, believing that all the natural intoxications of caresses would flow from her and not the barrel. . . ."[36] But ultimately, Djuna is not able to counter Rango's self-destructiveness with her loving attentiveness. After the *auto-da-fé* when he burns her books, the aphrodisiac lamp consumes all its oil, and Djuna confronts the reality that their relationship is doomed. An ironic and touching gloss on Nin's use of red is the fact that when Djuna was a child, she had created a paradise for herself under a library table covered with a red tablecloth. In her warm cave she read the forbidden books that belonged to her father. The nest under the table is similar to the love nest on the barge. By burning her books, Rango deprived Djuna of a personal world, of a precious source of consolation. This signifies the fact that their differences are insurmountable. Rango's fire, which once was a passion, becomes a destructive will to burn what is good. The reader now remembers that this character has been described as a dead volcano.

When the five novels are regarded as a single composition, *Cities of the Interior* may be compared to an abstract expressionist composition whose organization is dominated by huge areas of strong primary colors: yellow for Lillian who is exuberant and strong, garrulous, chaotic, passionate but inhibited; red for Sabina, a wild, dissatisfied woman who is always burning with unfulfilled desire; blue for the wise, reserved, self-controlled Djuna. These stand out against a more subtly colored background. Imagined in this way, the canvas seems to have been created by a series of improvisations. It is unfinished; it will lend itself to further elaboration, to the elimination of some elements and the addition of others, to redistribution of emphases, or even more drastic changes in the overall design.

With its open, dynamic form, a form that rejects the classical principle of self-enclosure or containment, *Cities of the Interior* is comparable, as well, to one of those sculptures found in museums of modern art which consist of several discrete parts that invite the spectator to participate in the composition by arranging these parts into a variety of patterns. The artist gives up his control over the work and offers to share the act of creation with the "audience." This comparison provides a good insight into the "continuous" structure of Nin's novel group, for the books do not at all require to be read in the order in which they were written (this order is reflected in the bound Swallow edition of 1959). It might be revealing to reverse this sequence, beginning with *Seduction* and arranging the other four novels to form a series of flashbacks to Lillian's flight from marriage and her difficult relationship with Jay. Another procedure might suggest pairing the two books that feature Lillian (*Ladders* and *Seduction*) with the two that feature Djuna (*Children* and *Heart*); these pairs are contrasting, and *Spy*, telling Sabina's story, could be placed in the center as a pivotal point that yields still more contrasts among the five books. Or, why not read *Spy* last instead of *Seduction?* As long as Nin's characters search for ways of expanding their lives and fusing various dimensions of their experience, there will be spaces for more "cities of the interior."[37]

Still another way of envisioning the structure of *Cities of the Interior* is musical. The lives of the three women are variations on a theme (the search for personal growth through relationships to people or to art). Each seeks this goal in her own way, at a different pace, and with different degrees of success. The personal rhythms of Nin's women are varied, so there is always novelty in reading about their private journeys. In an expanded context, then, the five novels are variations, each stating, developing, and redeveloping the central theme of Anaïs Nin's writing. Impressionistically speaking, the variations are differently colored: *Ladders* is vibrant and bold, brisk, crisply orchestrated, a wonderful contrast to the pale, luminous, glowing tone of *Children*. Heavy, damp, chilly, grey, *The Four-Chambered Heart* is a sort of *marche funèbre*. *A Spy in the House of Love* is like a streak of lightning until its mood changes toward the end when Sabina sinks to the floor of Djuna's studio like an exhausted bird. The coda is provided by *Seduction of the Minotaur*. This composition blends the elegiac mood of *The Four-Chambered Heart* with the brilliant sun-gold power that surges through the other books, animating their surfaces with hidden energy.

Nin's adoration of music connects her thought to modernism, on the one hand—particularly to Symbolism, as noted earlier—and on the other, it illuminates her personal vision of writing. One of the most persuasive discussions of the relationship between music and literature in the twentieth century is found in Walter Sokel's book *The Writer in Extremis*. Arguing that music has replaced sculpture as the primary art of the West, Sokel concludes that the abstract model provided by music means that "the framework of a poem, drama, or narrative would no longer have to be consistent with any external standard." Adopting the nonrepresentational, self-enclosed, and self-justifying language of music as an ideal of artistic expression, a writer attains freedom to depart from conventional realism which in the past obliged him to meet the spectator's "expectations based on his empirical experience." Art no longer need be either an imitation or an interpretation of empirical existence. It is free to express nothing external to itself; it is free to be an autonomous creation. Sokel calls this musicalization of the arts "the single most dominant characteristic of all modernism."[38]

The influence of music on Nin's symphonic style and natural unpredictable structures is more profound than that of either dance or painting. Music contributes to her themes and to her technique for displaying character, incident, and situation, as do the other arts; but in Nin's writing music also provides the controlling ideal of style and of structure. Her musical tastes are wide, ranging from folk music to the classics and the great moderns: Satie; Berg and Stravinsky. Edgar Varèse was a much-admired personal friend. One of her favorite composers is Debussy, whose art is close to Nin's own in mood, tone, color, and lyrical inventiveness. In the 1950s Nin became a great admirer of jazz whose patterns of improvisations and bold rhythms are distinctly heard in *Seduction of the Minotaur*.[39] Jazz has also influenced the language of later Diaries. Moreover, Nin, like many writers, often composed while listening to music. In August, 1935, she noted: "Writing more and more to the sound of music, writing more and more *like* music [italics mine]."[40] Ten years later she articulates what she means by "writing like music": "My symphonic writing puzzles those I love and trust. But I have had only the desire that writing should become music and penetrate the senses directly. For this, poetry is necessary. The unconscious speaks only the language of symbol. That is my language."[41]

In Nin's writing music is associated with a heightened sense of life, with moods of extreme intensity, emotional delicacy, or sensuous excitement. "There are various forms and states of ecstasy. Some are musical, one is possessed by sound, as if one lived inside of a vast bell."[42] Surely the most lyrical phallic symbol ever, a violin bow is used by a young woman in "The Voice" to create her own erotic music. Another type of consolation is offered by music in "Stella." The unhappy film star whose "hands preceded the ges-

ture of the body like some slender orchestra leader's baton un-
leashing a symphony," turns to music for a powerful counter force
against a telephone call she is determined not to answer. While the
phone rings she puts a concerto on the phonograph, for "In the
music there was a parallel to the conflict which disturbed her.
Within the concerto too the feminine and the masculine elements
were interacting." This music does not provide Stella with escape
from suffering; rather it presents her with a different expression of
conflict, educating her, elucidating a problem so that it loses its
"power to suck her back into the life with Bruno and the undertows
of suffering."[43] Again, Nin shows how art translates the lessons of
life into a smoothly seductive language that a sufferer can hear.

The most thoroughly musical of Nin's novels is *A Spy in the
House of Love*. The structure includes a controversial prelude; in
these pages Sabina telephones from a bar to a man called the lie
detector. Symbolically, she invites pursuit and discovery of her
crimes. Between the novel's prelude and its conclusion are presentations of Sabina's relationships with several men, each of whom is
associated with and characterized by an appropriate piece of music.
At the end Sabina moves into the consoling aura created by Djuna
who, always wise, calls upon Beethoven to instruct and inspire her
dejected friend.

The composition of *Spy* depends upon two interwoven patterns
of variation: the framing sections that probe Sabina's activities as
a "spy" and the enclosed, lyrically-wrought encounters with men.
The book's structure and style alike are musically inspired. The
"Firebird" is Sabina's "unerring musical autobiography." As well
as concealing a spy, Sabina's cape suggests the swirling motions of
flight. Significantly, the man who most tantalizes her, baffling and
frustrating her, is a former aviator. Sabina's eventual defeat is part
of the controlling metaphor of flight: "Sabina slid to the floor and
sat there with her head against the phonograph, with her wide skirt
floating for one instant like an expiring parachute; and then de-
flated completely and dying in the dust."[44] This image also suggests
the familiar fluttering movements of the dying swan in Tchaikow-
sky's ballet.

For Sabina love affairs are forms of adventure, of imaginative travel. Each man embodies an aura, a sense of place, a suggestion of a whole world of activity that lies waiting for her exploration and participation. In her state of illusory fusion with each man, Sabina imagines that she inhabits a new world, however briefly. First there is Philip. While sunbathing naked among the dunes on Long Island, Sabina is interrupted by Philip who is singing an aria from "Tristan and Isolde." Though attracted to him, Sabina is "haunted by the image of catastrophe, by the same obsessional forebodings which she heard in Ravel's Waltz."[45] Sabina and Philip sleep together, but she is left anguished and unsatisfied.

Disappointed in this particular quest for erotic experience, Sabina returns to her husband Alan. But his quiet, fatherly love is "murdered by the insistent, whispering, interfering dream, a compass pointing to mirages flowing in the music of Debussy like an endless beckoning, alluring. . . ."[46] *Clair de Lune* teases Sabina to pursue more adventures. Though she longs for Paris, the city of lovers, it is a hotter, more flamboyant place that next claims her. Alan brings Sabina a record of drumming and singing from the Ile Joyeuse. Ironically, Alan, whose work prevents him from taking Sabina there himself, inspires her dream of this particular voyage. It is enacted symbolically with Mambo, a black Greenwich Village drummer. Their relationship is doomed by a conflict between the reality of Mambo's life (a sick mother on the actual Ile Joyeuse and his awareness that Sabina pursues him in order to absorb an aura of the "primitive") and Sabina's fantasy of living the whole experience that she imagines to be connected with the Ile Joyeuse through her sexual relation to Mambo. He playfully but bitterly tests her by asking whether she would marry him and live there forever, accepting the care of his old, sick and, of course, black mother.

On Long Island, while waiting for Alan to get away from his work, Sabina meets John, the former aviator. But he has been wounded spiritually by his war experiences. He is convinced that sex is "bad." Their single encounter strangely haunts Sabina, but John is unwilling to repeat it. He flees from her. Sabina's disappointment deepens. Reminding her of the elusive John, Donald, a homosexual, is her next choice of companion: "Sabina had silenced the firebirds of desire, and now she extended her arms like widely extended wings, wings no longer orange, and Donald gave himself to their protective embrace."[47]

After Sabina's painful encounter with Jay, who in his painting displays his own exclusively sexual image of her, she is led away from Mambo's Night Club by Djuna. In her studio the two women silence the drums coming from the night club with a recording of a Beethoven quartet. This music is meditative, philosophical, expressive of a wisdom gained through suffering; it is the antidote to the provocative, exciting, disturbing but far less spiritual music that has possessed Sabina. The Beethoven quartet spins its message through a spiritual perspective on life that makes Sabina's personal sorrows seem insignificant. Consequently, she submits to a healing process. In this conclusion Nin dramatizes her own faith in music, suggesting that it is one means by which we can transcend our individual personal griefs and attain a more serene state of contemplation and regeneration.[48]

Music possesses spiritual power; it has a capacity to humanize emotions by expressing a plea for understanding and compassion. One of the most tender moments in Nin's fiction occurs in "Winter of Artifice"; the daughter is led toward forgiveness of her selfish father by a memory of her mother singing Schumann's *"J'ai pardonne."* The young woman reflects, "Strange how her mother, who had never forgiven her father, could sing that song more movingly than anything else she sang."[49] The daughter is a medium for feeling; her unconscious wish presents a memory as a spiritual instruction. Walking toward her father's house, she herself begins to sing *"J'ai pardonne."* This act of forgiveness is necessary not only for the father, whose weaknesses require redemption, but even more urgently for the daughter, who needs to be freed from guilt in order to pursue her own growth.

Above all, it is continuity that Nin associates with music and continuity that provides the basis of what she calls her "symphonic style" and her lyrically flowing structures. Music, like other expressions that affect the senses, evokes and transmits memory by the process of association of sensory images. The linking up of memories and of incidents from the past may not always bring pleasure, but it is always instructive, educating the feelings. In *The Four-Chambered Heart* a refrain from "Carmen" links something painful Djuna has experienced with Rango to something painful she experienced long ago with her father. She reflects: "If it were not for music, one could forget one's life and be born anew, washed of memories. If it were not for music one could walk through the markets of Guatemala, through the snows of Tibet, up the steps of Hindu temples, one could change costumes, shed possessions, retain nothing of the past. But music pursues one. . . ." Sometimes the message that is transmitted communicates joy: "Diana's laughter was continuous, so that it seemed, like the music of the guitars, an accompaniment to their days in Golconda." At the close of *Children* Djuna has suffered and has survived a near drowning; now she must descend into herself for enlightenment and fortification, for the initiation and preparation that will precede a new relationship, a new phase of her life:

> Djuna walked back again into her labyrinthian cities of the interior.

> Where music bears no titles, flowing like a subterranean river carrying all the moods, sensations and impressions into dissolutions forming and reforming a world in terms of flow . . . .

Temporarily, she leaves behind her sense of her individual self:

> but Djuna knew that at this surrender of the self began a sinking into deeper layers of awareness, deeper and deeper starting at the topsoil of gaiety and descending through the geological stairways carrying only the delicate weighing machine of the heart to weigh the imponderable

Djuna knew too

> that only the important dates of deep feeling may recur again and again each time anew through the wells, fountains and rivers of music. . . .[50]

Nin's "symphonic writing" rises from the depths of the psyche to emerge to consciousness in fountains of revelation, underground power made visible in jets of disclosure, analysis, or evocative re-creation of characters, scenes, situations, and meditative passages. The power of this flowing style is the way in which it collects and organizes, even as it streams along, the diverse materials of which life is composed: its fragments; odds and ends; remnants; all the seemingly unimportant or discarded scraps that Nin reassembles into new forms. Once again—as always—compassion is the focus of Nin's art. As Nin matured she grew into the conviction that it is not enough for the artist to perform the alchemical magic of simply transforming the ugly into the beautiful. The artist must articulate the dreams of the mute. The artist must, also, like Proust, record the "eternal moments." And, ironically, though Djuna's words can-not do this, Nin's words can:

> But no words came as one of Beethoven's Quartets began to tell Sabina, as Djuna could not, of what they both knew for absolute certainty: the continuity of existence and of the chain of summits, of elevations by which such continuity is reached. By elevation the consciousness reached a perpetual move-ment, transcending death, and in the same manner attained the continuity of love by seizing upon its impersonal essence, which was a summation of all the alchemies producing life and birth, a child, a work of art, a work of science, a heroic act, an act of love.[51]

The Dream

Everyone says: you must take sides, choose a political party,
choose a philosophy, choose a dogma. . . . I chose the dream
of human love.

—*The Four-Chambered Heart*

In Anaïs Nin's writing perhaps no word appears so frequently in
so many contexts or with so many nuances as the word "dream."
Nin's vision of the dream gives continuity and profundity to her
meaning as woman and artist alike. Dream provides the controlling image of unity and transformation in her fiction; it provides
the major theme of *The Novel of the Future,* and it is the subject
of several of the talks collected in *A Woman Speaks.* Her belief in
the positive nature of the unconscious has given Nin many valuable
insights. Even more importantly, it has given her processes for healing that range from the discoveries and consolations of psychoanalysis to a philosophy of creation that connects a theory of the development of the self with that of the artist. Although Nin's concept of the dream has altered slightly as she has experienced her
life, it remains basically a vision of human love. "I dance, I sew, I
mend, I cook for the sake of this dream. In this dream nobody dies,
nobody is sick, nobody separates. I love and dance with my dream
unfurled, trusting darkness, trusting the labyrinth, into the fur-
naces of love."[1] In devotion to the dream of love fulfilled, Nin is as
fastidious and compassionate as in her thriftiness toward experience, the quality that makes her, like Varda, a collage-maker. There

is an unrecognized pragmatist in Nin. Her dreams are never idle fantasies. They must be *used*, as *House of Incest* is a book made from dreams. In *The Novel of the Future* Nin points out that she begins every piece of writing with a dream. It is the passivity of the drug-user that Nin condemns in contrast to the activity of the creator who uses his dreams in his work. Also, in addition to providing the material of art as well as the inspiration, dreams are a form of communication. Dreams can nourish and influence one another. Dreams *make things happen,* Nin says. They are not only part of reality, they shape reality. "You see, psychoanalysis gives you a sense of reality—and I don't mean in terms of accepting something lower or of less quality than what you wanted—but in terms of how to fulfill it. What I really learned was how to attain these things that I really wanted and that they were not impossible."[2] Put more succinctly and amusingly, Nin writes: "I go in to come out.'[3]

Nin's love of the artist is matched in intensity and devotion by her love of the physician and healer. Four psychoanalysts are perceptively and affectionately portrayed in the Diaries: Drs. Allendy, Rank, Jaeger, and Bogner. In *Collages* a Dr. Mann, along with Renate, rescues the lonely writer, Judith Sands. Early in her life when Nin feared losing her artist's temperament, her dreamy and poetic nature in the ruthless exposure of psychoanalysis, she wrote with relief of Rank that she had "found in the world of psychoanalysis the only metaphysical man in it." She adds, "I lived out the poem and came out unscathed. Free. A poet still."[4] The analysts whom she worked with later in her continuous goal of self-liberation receive a respect that is undamaged by Nin's own ability to analyze them from her personal point of view. This is natural, for Nin, who rejected conventional schools, has chosen her own educators from among artists and doctors. Psychoanalysis has been her school of continuing education, and she has many times attributed her growth to this therapy. Once, despite her love of artists, she wrote, "The psychologists are doing the only constructive work in the world."[5] She has paid tribute to Rank not only in her Diary and her speeches but also in the tender characterization found in "The Voice." *Diaries V* and *VI* contain a continuous admiring portrait of the brilliant and compassionate psychoanalyst, Inge Bogner. An austere and tragic yet appealing healer is Dr. Hernandez who appears in *Seduction of the Minotaur;* he is the man who guides Lillian toward self-understanding with his penetrating questions. Djuna, too, is dedicated to healing the confused or wounded friends who come to her. While Nin values and admires doctors, she is critical of the ones who are indifferent to suffering, as in the "Birth" story, or who place their own convenience before their patients' needs. In *Seduction of the Minotaur* the cynical Dr. Palas is contrasted to the compassionate Dr. Hernandez, who dies trying to protect the Indians who are his patients from narcotics' smugglers.

Nin's admiration for artists and doctors alike arises from the fact that both are devoted to the protection of life. They are warriors in an eternal battle against decay and, finally, death. Their profound involvement with the extreme and universal states of birth and death leads them into the depths of experience that Nin believes must be explored if we are to achieve the conscious awareness and the control that make growth possible. In "The Writer and the Symbols," Nin expresses her view that "Few aside from doctors and a few novelists have been willing to plunge into the unexplored territory of our irrational life."[6]

This "unexplored territory," of course, is the unconscious. Jung himself is poetic when he describes the unconscious as ". . . everything of which I know, but of which I am not at the moment thinking; everything of which I was once conscious but have now forgotten; everything perceived by my senses, but not noted by my conscious mind; everything which, involuntarily and without paying attention to it, I feel, think, remember, want, and do; all the future things that are taking shape in me and will sometime come to consciousness: all this is the content of the unconscious."[7] The language of the unconscious is the dream: "ideas and images in the mind *not under the command of reason."* One does not have to be asleep to dream. This activity "may include reverie, imagination, daydreaming—visions and hallucinations under the influence of drugs—any experience which emerges from the realm of the subconscious."[8] The dream serves many purposes. One can make of it a self-sustaining world severed from consciousness, a counterworld that is exciting in itself, as it was for the Surrealists, simply because it is so different from familiar reality. Dreams can represent a substitute for reality. For Sabina and Djuna, too, the reality of love replaces the dream. Dreams complement the conscious life, enriching it, filling out empty spaces, providing opportunities for expression of impulses that have been repressed. In this sense dream is indispensable as the compensatory process that maintains our sanity. Another attribute of dream is its power of revelation, one that is relative because of the symbolic nature of dream language. The adventurous and skillful interpreter of visual imagery may discover himself—past, present, and future. While learning to unravel mysteries, he may uncover the source of personal problems, recognize his true desires, or gain the courage to explore hidden talents and aspirations. He may even discover himself: "Within each of us there is another whom we do not know. He speaks to us in dreams. . . ."[9]

On a less personal, a universal level, dreams show how we are related to other men not only in the present but in ancient times when the archetypal patterns of today were also presenting themselves in the symbolic dramas of myth, folk literature, and dreams. There is, finally, the common, perhaps the most ordinary meaning of "dream"—to represent a wonderful or marvelous ideal, a desire—whether material or spiritual—that seems impossible to attain, be it as trivial as a marvelous dress or as profound as a vision of divine love.

In Nin's career, dreams have, at various times, possessed all these types of significance. Dreams have provided her with extraordinary ideals: those of total personal liberty and creative self-expression; a vision of mankind's liberation from hostile and destructive impulses through self-awareness; and the transformation of negative energies into productive actions. Finally, as a form of symbolic expression, the dream has been invaluable to Anaïs Nin as she gradually developed her personal language and her philosophy of poetic writing.

A shared fascination with the strangeness of images flowing from the unconscious links Nin to the Surrealists, who saw in this raw power a means of creating a revolutionary super-reality. With the Surrealists, too, particularly with André Breton, Nin shares a faith in the relationship of man and woman through eroticism and passion. But in other respects, Nin's view of how dream can be used in art differs from the Surrealists' ideal of "pure psychic automatism." In *Diary III* and in *The Novel of the Future* Nin praises the Surrealists for emphasizing man's need for liberty and for locating the source of this liberty in the unconscious. At the same time, she criticizes their insistence on presenting the raw contents of the unconscious, the results of automatic writing, without interpreting them. "What the surrealists did was to situate themselves within the unconscious and not relate it to action. They cut the umbilical cord. But in antique cultures the dream was a part of life itself, influenced it. Everyone was engaged in unraveling the mysterious dreams which were an indication of a psychic life."[10] Because they refused to make the interpretive connections, Nin claims that the Surrealists often produced a rigid, artificial art; even more dangerous, by isolating themselves within the unconscious they risked insanity, a tragic condition that Nin portrayed in her sketch of Pierre (Artaud) in "Je suis le plus Malade des Surréalistes." Writers must not simply present the contents of their unconscious lives; in Nin's view they are responsible for showing why these materials are meaningful. "Some writers have brought the irrational streams into visibility but like reporters unable to extract either philosophical or psychological deductions from their findings, they emptied their vast nets filled with chaos and threw debris and absurd juxtapositions at our feet . . . I am thinking now of many of the surrealist writers."[11]

Nin's ideal of symphonic writing has as its source not only what she has learned from the nonverbal arts but also what she has discovered from her lifelong trust in and perceptive observation of dreams. In particular the dream has given her a personalized approach to the creation of fictional characters, along with certain convictions about the structure and language that have by now become accepted tenets of twentieth-century thought. Her experience with psychoanalysis gave Nin personal proof of Bergson's theoretical and Proust's esthetic views of space, time and personality. Like the theory of relativity, which was made public at about the same time as Freud's *Interpretation of Dreams,* dreams show how time and space have meaning only when fused; they are not themselves reality but ways of orienting oneself toward it. Imagination and memory easily transcend literal demarcations in space and time. Clock time is arbitrary; it is merely a convenience, designed by man to organize his day within the periodic alternations of nature. Each space or place carries within it an individual experience of time. The site of true time is the subterranean dimension of each individual. Each moves through life at his own private rhythm, seeking to harmonize his personal pace with the external rhythms of the groups in which he needs or wishes to move. Consequently, each of us lives in several time zones simultaneously: there are those of our race, our culture, our nation, our family, the chronological time we use to organize our daily lives and the personal internalized patterns that we can discover only by learning to interpret our waking and sleeping dreams. Nin often refers to these personal dimensions of time and of space as "relativity." "Changes occur constantly according to the vision, image, or myth which possesses one. We do not grow absolutely, chronologically. We grow sometimes in one dimension, and not in another, unevenly. We grow partially. We are relative. We are mature in one realm, childish in another. The past, present and future mingle and pull us backward, forward, or fix us in the present."[12]

The great importance placed by psychologists on the unconscious is the single most influential factor in Nin's approach to characterization. Once the practice and the prevalence of repression were discovered by Freud and other investigators of the psyche, along with the ways in which people inadvertently express their real desires through "slips" of the tongue, accidents, physical symptoms, and other indirect expressions of emotion, it became clear that the way people dress and behave, even the things they say and do are not always accurate expressions of their selves. The surfaces that are reproduced by conventional novelists are misleading, for they may actually be the costumes, the disguises behind which the real people are hiding. The process of socialization which exposes individuals to the pressures of family and environment forces people to adopt a series of *personae* or masks.[13] The goal of Nin's fiction is the portrayal of her characters' hidden selves. She achieves this not with continuous linear description, but by portraying them quickly but repeatedly at certain highly selective moments. During times of extreme pressure or crisis when defenses are weak, true feelings burst through the protective facade of the *persona*. Nin's characters are caught for the reader in a series of revelations. Together, these make a composite; in that way several swift glances portray a character through superimposed images, much as Duchamp does in the famous portrait of the nude moving down the staircase, an image which Nin borrowed to depict Sabina in *A Spy in the House of Love*.

Nin's emphasis on states of feeling and awareness has meant that her readers miss such familiar guides in traditional characterization as family names, ages, occupations, places of residence, and similar details of surface. Emphatically denying some reviewers' charges that she writes "case studies" because of the psychological orientation of her work—Nin concedes that her characters are abstract, while reserving the privilege of defining the term herself. She says that "to abstract" means to extract the essence of her subject, eliminating whatever merely renders the surface.[14] Nin never relates anything about a character simply because it is there to be observed. She selects the details that are the most expressive, the most telling, restricting these to a small number; then as she proceeds to make her shots of each character, she composes patterns and variations upon the details she has selected. Sabina's swirling cape, so admired by other women, suggests the costume of a spy in melodramatic fiction or film: it is glamorous and mysterious, but, above all, the cape expresses her need for concealment. Lillian's choked energy and unrealized capacity for passion are expressed by her way of dressing: "Tumult in orange, red and yellow and green quarreling with each other. The rose devoured the orange, the green and blue overwhelmed the purple. The sport jacket was irritated to be in company with the silk dress, the tailored coat at war with the embroidery, the everyday shoes at variance with the turquoise bracelet. And if at times she chose a majestic hat, it sailed precariously like a sailboat on a choppy sea."[15] The revealing gestures, the unexpected tone of voice, the angle of a head, the choice of an unusual word; to the sensitive observer these reveal truths. Her ear adjusted to these half-tones, Nin has brought a highly original approach to characterization: "I am not writing case histories . . . Psychoanalysis is merely the basic philosophy of my work. I accept its premise, that it is the unconscious which rules and shapes our lives. I am making a new art of storytelling, not stories told as case histories, but stories told with a new vision of the unfolding of character."[16]

The nature of this new vision is poetic; it depends not upon description and narration, nor upon dramatization, as in traditional fiction, but upon the patterned presentation of symbolic materials. Plot and linear structure disappear in Nin's compositions. They are formal arrangements based upon repetitions, contrasts, similarities, or variations composed around basic themes. In Nin's work everything is symbolic, sometimes even the characters themselves. Like many other modern writers, Nin mixes levels or modes of reality. Purely symbolic satiric figures like the Chess Player or Faustin the Zombie or Cold Cuts are employed now and then, partly as shorthand reminders of the social world in which the novel is set, but more importantly as quick comments or glosses on the central characters. These flattened-out figures represent significant aspects of the main characters.

The most controversial figure of this type is the lie detector whom Sabina telephones at the beginning of *A Spy in the House of Love*. *Diary V* recounts Nin's battles with friends and publishers who protested against this "unrealistic" opening. Nin's deep understanding of psychology and of personality gave her a strong defense: "I was shocked, shocked by the unanimous dislike for the lie detector. René de Chocor [Nin's agent at the time] said: 'He should not be a personage, even mythical. It is her guilt and should be inside of her.' But I know how often we project our guilt outside of us, to the policeman, father, confessor, husband, doctor, analyst, critical friend or art critic! The projection creates the hallucination of condemnation in the eyes of others. Sabina being neurotic and primitive, or subjective, would see this outside of herself, personified." In a letter to de Chocor, Nin declared: "If the novel fails now, *tant pis*. There is no place for the poetic novel anyway. I would rather sink with it as it is and with my feeling of integrity. I am being true to a new form which will evolve out of the new relativity of psychological reality."[17]

The use of the lie detector is in perfect harmony with Nin's technique of employing minor characters as projections of emotions felt but not recognized by major characters, a technique that first appears in *House of Incest*. Though the lie detector has no importance in himself, and Sabina's phoning him is in a literal sense impossible, the incident sets the tone for the novel by expressing Sabina's terror, the feverish, haunted, frantic atmosphere of a quest that fails the more decisively as it gains in desperation. Considered together with the final scene of confession and self-recognition, the opening telephone call to the lie detector universalizes Sabina's experience, extending its significance far beyond her personal failure. Whether Sabina *could* have phoned such a man would be a legitimate question in a "realistic novel"; here the question itself betrays a lack of understanding of Nin's method of writing lyrical psychological fiction rooted in a conviction that virtually everything is symbolic of a hidden truth. Just as the character of Mathilda in *Children of the Albatross* is meant to represent Djuna's own unconscious isolation from men, so Djuna herself is symbolic of one aspect of woman, her power of compassionate perception.

One of the most common complaints against Nin's fiction is that her characters are "all herself." To voice this as a negative feeling is to reveal a misunderstanding of how characters in fiction are created; all are projections of some part of the author's self. It would be more to the point to criticize a novelist for drawing shallow characterizations based more nearly on observation than on empathy and emotional understanding. The women of *Cities of the Interior* are individuals; yet each symbolizes an aspect of woman:

"Djuna, perception [it is she who bears the closest resemblance to Nin's public self]; Stella, blind suffering; Sabina, the free woman; Lillian, the one who seeks freedom in aggression."[18] Nin's characters are perfectly individualized; if it were not for the published Diaries readers would not be able to compare the author with her created characters. If we were to read the Diaries of all novelists we would see that the process of creating fictional personages from the unlived parts of the author's self is a familiar and basic process. Nin's portraits are both detailed and profound, for they simultaneously express the individual and the collective dimensions: "We enter the deepest, most hidden realm of all, a region unacknowledged, where all women melt into one, and only in that moment of hopeless struggle to free one's self of one absolute love are all women melted into one. It is in the night life, in the unconscious, that this resemblance takes place . . ."[19]

Again, dream is the teacher, providing a model of the way in which the psyche divides itself into separate parts when we involuntarily enact the symbolic dramas of the night. It is not an exaggeration to claim that all the figures of our dreams represent aspects of ourselves, the desires, emotions, fears, that we have driven into the unconscious by our refusal to recognize them. But because they are strong and authentic, these aspects of ourselves become active when consciousness relaxes its power of censorship. Freed, they symbolically express whatever it was we could not allow ourselves to experience in the brightness of day. Nin's approach to characterization reflects this process. Familiar with the intense personal content of dreams as well as the way in which the ego seeks to complete itself through identifications with others in friendship or love, she has made her characters deeper than do writers who deny the importance of the unconscious or condemn it because of its "irrational" nature. In this Nin emulates Proust: "What irony that Proust who selected the most shallow of all people, the wealthy and aristocratic, should have reached the greatest depths which a novelist has reached into the unconscious, and that he was accused of depicting only decadents. He created the best portrait of a servant, Francoise, better than that of any social realist, like Zola or Balzac. I can't remember any of Zola's or Balzac's characters, yet I know all of Proust's intimately."[20]

The rich, sometimes dark and sometimes dazzling dreams that rise from the unconscious animate and inspire the imagination. As Gaston Bachelard writes in *The Poetics of Reverie,* the Jungian view is powerful because "For Jung, the subconscious self is not a repressed consciousness, it is not made of forgotten memories; it is a *primary nature* [italics mine]."[21] Works of art are, as Nin has said, "articulate dreams." They are visions that the artist has made public by translating a private symbolism into significant form and by animating a personal drama with the energy of powerful feeling and intelligence. Like rivers, dreams are a process that can be envisioned as a flow. From this ceaseless flowing motion the artist lifts the moments that possess special significance for him. After transforming these and interpreting them with his own language of colors, notes, or words, he returns his private obsessions to the stream of existence in the form of poetic expressions.

Dreams provide transcendence. This is why Nin so frequently refers to Rank's theory of creative will, as described in *Will Therapy* and *Truth and Reality,* why she insists that psychoanalysis can be a philosophy, and why she has always insisted on the practical nature of the dream. It must be used, welded to life, brought into relationships of mutual exchange and influence if it is to be a creative power.

Nin has not always held an unqualifiedly positive view of the dream. At first there was dream as nightmare, for which the French word *cauchemar* is so expressive. To submit to the nightmare is to be locked into a prison where revelations are inescapable, worse still, terrifying with their message of unrelieved truth. In *House of Incest* Nin writes, "I walked into my own book seeking peace. It was night, and I made a careless movement inside the dream; I turned too brusquely the corner and I bruised myself against my madness."[22] The prison of a dream, however, need not be terrifying or harmful; it may instead provide the narcotic of escape, an ease of living unknown or unattainable to the dreamer in his waking life. Fantasy can provide all that life withholds. In "The Voice,"

Djuna acknowledges the irresistible allure of the dream as a counterworld where passivity provides an alternative to control and discipline, even to perceptive emotional awareness: "Awareness hurts. Relationships hurt. Life hurts. But to float, to drift, to live in the dream does not hurt."[23]

Nin has called her last work of fiction a "collage of dreamers." With experience she had come to value fantasy for its healing powers. She does not condemn the dreamers of *Collages.* Some of them are simply not strong enough to seize what they want in life; for these dreamers, fantasy is merciful in fulfilling precious desires. But for other people, the stronger ones, the dream offers transforming insights; it is a school for the emotions. Again, Nin is, in her winsome way, a pragmatist. Dreams must be used, and to be used they must be connected to life. Just as she criticizes the Surrealists for presenting the raw materials of their psyches without interpretation or translation, she repeatedly declares in *The Novel of the Future, A Woman Speaks* and in her essay collection, that dreams have no value until they have been brought into relation with life, of which they are an essential part. In Nin's later work the emphasis on the dream shifts from its compensatory role to its power of extending experience into the mysterious but enthralling world of the unconscious. Previously unknown or inaccessible areas of feeling and knowledge become open to the dreamer whose spirit of adventure liberates him from the restrictive confines, from the myopic world view of empiricism. The bold dreamer is a traveler in the foreign, sometimes frightening or shocking, and sometimes miraculous territory of the psyche. To dream is to know and to experience vastly more than when one is awake. Sometimes this knowledge changes one. In Djuna Barnes' *Nightwood,* a book that Nin loved, the generous Nora confesses: " 'I used to think that people just went to sleep, or if they did not go to sleep that they were themselves, but now—' she lit a cigarette and her hands trembled—'now I see that the night does something to a person's identity, even when asleep.' " In the process of comforting her, the doctor delivers a fantastic oration on the night, asserting that ' ". . . the tree of night is the hardest tree to mount, the dourest tree to scale, the most difficult of branch, the most febrile to the touch, and sweats a resin and drips a pitch against the palm that computation has not gambled.' "[24]

But Dr. Matthew Mighty-grain-of-salt-Dante O'Connor views dreams as trees to be mounted. The association between dream and motion is central to Nin's thought. To dream is to live; to live obligates one to accept a life of fluidity and motion. Nin calls psychology a "philosophy of mobility."[25] A metaphysician of imagery, Bachelard, for example, could write an entire book based on the metaphor of motion in Nin's writing. Dreaming is mental traveling; it is available to the adventurous imagination. But courage is also needed to permit the daring dreamer to enter the labyrinth of self. To find one's way in the dark twisting corridors of the unconscious, one needs a guide. What the guide provides is awareness, interpretive intelligence, the faculty that translates imagery into understanding. The guide may be the psychoanalyst, the physician (as Dr. Hernandez serves Lillian as therapist), or it may be a wise, perceptive friend. It is Djuna, often referred to as Ariadne, who leads her friends and lovers out of the darkness of their ignorance of themselves toward clarity, lucidity, toward understanding of the reasons for their suffering.

The four elements provide one sort of metaphor in Nin's fiction; they are at the same time associated with motion of different kinds and significance. Transcendence is, naturally, connected with rising or flying. In *House of Incest* it is specifically ascension that represents this metaphysical direction, and ascension is terrifying to the neurotic "I" whose entrance into the "house of incest" (self-absorption, self-love, neurotic obsession) is the adventure of the book. But in later works Nin has overcome the fear of ascension. She dreams of herself as a rocket streaking to the moon. "I feel a tension which should carry me to the moon." There is no fear here, rather excitement and expectation. In *Diary II* she praises Blaise Cendrars for wanting "to be the first man to fly to the moon."[26]

The flights that attract Nin are night flights. They are voyages to the moon.[27] Flight unites the most ancient of man's ambitions with the most contemporary conquests of the space age. The archetype of flight is connected with fecundation, the implanting of the new, concepts, visions, ideals, with revelations of worlds beyond this one. Sabina's moon baths bring her visions of expansion: "Now she began to see the forms and colors of other lives, realms much deeper and stranger and remote to be discovered, and that her denial of ordinary life had a purpose: to send her off like a rocket into other forms of existence." Moonrays germinate in her "the power to extend time in the ramifications of myriad lives and loves, to expand the journey to infinity, taking immense and luxurious detours as the courtesan depositor of multiple desires."[28] As Nin's work has become more comprehensive and more mature, there is a greater force of synthesis; so her most profound book, *Seduction of the Minotaur,* contains accommodations both for night journeys and journeys by daylight, both a lunar barque and a solar barque.

Flight is complemented by the recurrent image of flowing, an image which also expresses Nin's aspirations for her writing style. One of her notebooks for 1936 was titled "Les Mots Flottants." The flowing motion is synonymous with living naturally without resistance to change. When one is flowing he experiences simultaneous contact with the three elements of water, earth, and air. However, it is very difficult to achieve the motion of flowing; and often there are obstacles to the attainment of this ideal state of being. Very often Nin's characters are frustrated; there are all sorts of impediments for the boats she writes about. In "Winter of Artifice" just before the arrival of the father she has not seen for twenty years, the daughter breaks a crystal bowl that contains a glass ship. Misinterpreting this in the context of her hopes, she concludes that in finding him again she may have found her port at last. In reality, it is another journey that awaits her. The breaking of the bowl frees the water as the daughter's gradual reappraisal of her father frees her from her childish fantasy of creating a life with him; she is now ready to journey into her own future as a woman. In other books there are descriptions of stranded ships: the ship on land; the ship exiled to a cemetery for barges; the ship that leaks. All suggest some interference with the motion of life.

In *The Novel of the Future,* when Nin wants to show how dreams influence and actually cause actions, she discloses the source of her desire to live in a houseboat. In Etretat in Brittany she visited a house that was once occupied by De Maupassant. In the garden was a fishing boat that had been washed ashore. "The boat in the Maupassant garden left high and dry, unable to sail any more, stirred the memory of the recurrent dream. To exorcise the dream, or fulfill it, I sought a real houseboat and lived in it (also dreamt in it)."[29] The houseboat receives its tribute in the sketch of the same title found in *Under a Glass Bell*. Later, the houseboat becomes a barge moored in the Seine; it is a love nest for lovers whose attraction is doomed. This boat moves, but only to sink. In Nin's later works the boats are usually freer to move because the characters themselves are more mobile. Bruce and Renate's barge navigates the rivers and canals of central Europe but only because Renate assumes the responsibility of bailing; this is of course a comment on their relationship. The most dignified and metaphysically suggestive use of boats is found in *Seduction of the Minotaur* when Lillian and Dr. Hernandez drift in a jungle lagoon. Their hand-carved canoe made from a tree trunk reminds Lillian of the solar barque which the ancient Egyptians placed in tombs to carry them to the moon; the solar barque was for travel by day, the lunar barque for the night journey. Here, the boat is a figure of connection, uniting and drawing together seemingly opposed realms.

The position of the dream at the center of Nin's art may be wonderfully illustrated by looking at one of her most brilliant pieces, "The Voice." Here the dream is truly a vehicle of mobility. "The Voice" is a virtuoso piece that spins off from contrasting motions: soaring, plummeting, floating, sinking, spiraling, rushing, or flowing, along a horizontal or lying quietly on a bed to daydream. This thoughtful work is neither a story nor a sketch, but an animated essay or exposition of ideas through a seemingly random selections of characters and incidents. The center is a psychoanalysts's office located in a skyscraper (suggestive of the Empire State Building or one of the structures at Rockefeller Center). Most of the characters are presented to the reader through the compassionate vision of Djuna, who analyzes the analyst himself, The Voice. Tortured New Yorkers all, The Voice's patients include, besides

Djuna herself: a young violinist who wishes to be released from her lesbianism; Mischa, a cellist whose childhood experiences have paralyzed his emotions; Lilith, who suffers from frigidity; The Voice himself who, appealingly, falls in love with Lilith, the only one of his patients who can see beyond her own needs to the hungers of the man whose voice is so comforting to the others. As in later works, Djuna plays the role of confidante to both parties in this unwise and ultimately impossible dream of romantic love between analyst and patient.

The portraits of the patients and their progress with The Voice are enclosed or framed by opening and closing meditations that unite the concept of motion with the idea of the dream. Like *Collages,* "The Voice" is composed of many short sections; there are fifteen. The first and second comprise Djuna's meditations on movement and growth, while the third, fourth, and fifth depict The Voice working with his patients. In the sixth the focus is returned to Djuna, who after an initial ascent to the top of the building now finds herself in an underground drugstore with others whom the city has "swallowed." A more terrifying descent still is reported: the suicide of a woman pregnant with a five-month child but without anyone to love her. The seventh, eighth, and ninth episodes are concerned with Lilith's overly intense relationship with her brother (another appearance of the incest theme in Nin's work) and her immature dream that love for The Voice may free her from this past entanglement. The tenth passage is again Djuna's. It is a rhapsody, a vision of identification with the moon which since time immemorial has been thought to control the cyclic life of woman through her physiology. "Djuna was one with the moon, thrusting hands made of roots into the storm, while her heart beat like a drum through the orgy of the moonstorm." By contrast, Lilith still struggles, suffering from a headache, finding that "the seed would not burst; the body left the earth, pulled upward by a string of nerves and spilled its pollen only in space . . ."[30] Lilith cannot release herself into storms of emotion as Djuna has done in her vision.

The twelfth and thirteenth portions of "The Voice" explore Lilith's frigidity and her sorrow. Like other characters to follow,

Lilith seeks refuge in Djuna. Between women there is not the
tension of polarity that troubles relationships between men and
women, the more so as they are individuals burdened with emotional problems. Lilith understands, finally, that it is self-defeating
to be in love with The Voice. Knowing that she must free herself
from him as a doctor, for this is part of her treatment, Lilith has
fantasized a love for the healer as a man, imagining that this would
enable her to hold onto him. "But when he was not being the doctor, she discovered, he was not a man but a child." Growth means
discarding illusions about others as well as reaching for independence. Lilith accepts the fact that "neither her powers of illusion
nor her dreams had worked the miracle. He remained nothing but
A VOICE."[31] In this relationship Nin has traced the well-known
process of transference, but the sensitivity, the fineness of perception, and gentle humor with which she has done it altogether transform the clinical situation into a skillfully fictionalized one. She
has made the parties to a therapeutic relationship sympathetic, vulnerable human beings.

Though there are references in "The Voice" to the identification
of the dream with flowing motion, this piece emphasizes the contrasting rhythms of rising and falling, or ascending and descending. In the Hotel Chaotica, Djuna envisions "hysteria and darkness,
wells, prisons, tombs." "Lying down in a cell-shaped room," she
imagines the rapid movements of the elevators whose passengers
are trapped between the top and bottom floors of the hotel. "The
people riding up and down the elevators are never permitted to
crash through the last ceiling into pure space and never allowed to
pierce through the ground floor to enter the demonic regions below the crust of the earth."[32] They are trapped in the reality of the
hotel, a mundane reality that reaches neither toward the heavens
nor toward the lower infernal regions. Djuna alone is able to navi-
gate these regions through the forceful propulsion of her imagination.

Counterpointed against the constant rising and falling of the
elevator is the horizontal rush of pedestrians along New York's
crowded streets. After each patient leaves the analyst, he experi-

ences a charge of liberation, a great release that enables him to do or to feel something that was formerly impossible because of the inhibitions of neurosis. Djuna, for example, has been fighting a desire to remain still, to refuse motion and change, but "suddenly she began walking faster than whoever was walking beside her, to feel the exultation of passing them. The one who does not move feels abandoned, and the one who loves and weeps and yields feels he is living so fast the debris cannot catch up with him." The young woman violinist drops to the sidewalk to pray. Mischa is flooded with warmth and fire that cause him to burst out in song. Lilith comes upon a rare sense of harmony: "She was breathing with the day, moving with the wind, in accord with it, with the sky, undulating like water, flowing and stirring to the life about her, opening like the night.[33]

These moments of spontaneous expression balance the terrifying descent that occurs near the middle of "The Voice," the suicide of the pregnant woman who jumps from the roof of the hotel. Perhaps she could have saved herself if she had allowed her dreams to carry her beyond this roof, or ceiling, in transcendence. Immediately after the dull thud of her falling body there is a renewal of motion and activity. Since the characters in "The Voice" are patients in analysis, the woman's suicide is especially ominous. To reassure themselves they immediately begin to move in countermotion horizontally. "One must get dizzy. One must move. Move." This theme is underscored when Lilith goes to the harbor to meet her brother whom she has not seen since childhood. Their meeting draws her back into the past toward an encounter with the origin of her neurosis. She and her brother are said to "sail inside the static sea of their fantasies."[34] Neurosis is a fixation on some person or situation from the past. The cure is to step inside the dream, allowing it to carry one downward toward self-discovery or upward toward release, exhilaration, toward the freedom of soaring into space. But this rising and falling motion must be balanced with the horizontal stream or flow of life in which one lets oneself be carried along with others, mixing with them, taking part in the communal as well as in the private and purely personal life.

With passing years the idea of the dream has matured as the inner life of the writer has developed. Without losing any of its importance, the dream has been woven more deeply into the fabric of Nin's writing. The emphasis increasingly is placed on the power of the dream to lead us more deeply into life and to fuse its various dimensions. The dreamer herself moves away from the solitary states of the early years toward a recognition of the universal or archetypal nature of certain essential symbols: "What I condemn now is not my tendency to live by my imagination, but the fact that I did not always see that when I concretized a fantasy (as for example the houseboat) it was not a single, unique isolated experience . . . this unconscious myth had been dreamed by other men as they dream of desert islands, the heart of Africa, sailing a boat alone. . . ." While it is true that dreams are a source of personal consolation and revelation, they also show man's connections with other men. The author begins to caution her readers against confusing dreams with reality, against seeking them as drugs, means of escape, flights from the present: "What turned me away from romanticism (neurosis in modern terms) was an obsession with the far in place of the near, with the unattainable in place of the attainable . . . Romanticism became clearly synonymous with neurosis."[35]

In Lillian's journey to Mexico and her confrontation with herself Nin creates a living dream simultaneously in the past, present and future. *Seduction of the Minotaur* wonderfully displays Nin's delicate sense of structure while also bringing to maturity an idea touched upon in *A Spy in the House of Love*. The meaning of freedom is not flight, as Sabina imagines, but commitment. If a woman can discover and love the many aspects of a man, she can be content with one love. Sabina's blindness to all but the single face that suits her fantasy condemns her to fly from one man to another. In *Seduction of the Minotaur* Lillian learns the lesson Sabina cannot absorb; Lillian learns to see Larry, from whom she has been separated, as a complex, multidimensional person. This discovery brings a new excitement, a forgiveness, the grace of understanding to her feelings about him. Because she untangles the knot of her own past, she rediscovers her love of her husband.

Like Hesse's *Demian* and *Steppenwolf, Seduction of the Minotaur* is a poetically treated psychoanalysis projected through a series of symbolic encounters. In Nin's book these encounters superimpose crucial moments in past and present time, moments which are significant for the future. Lillian has grown; she is freer. Now a jazz, rather than classical, pianist, Lillian visits Golconda in Mexico where she has an engagement at the Black Pearl night club. She seeks a unity with Mexico itself, a suspension between past and future in a soothing, languid present. But immediately Doctor Hernandez, who is much like the portrait of Otto Rank in "The Voice," challenges her to confront herself. He accuses Lillian of acting like a "fugitive." Lillian counters with resistance. But in fact from the moment early in the novel when she enters the solar barque with Dr. Hernandez, Lillian has committed herself to a double journey; her exploration of Mexico in present time leads her into subterranean passages of memory, her personal labyrinth where she relives crucial childhood experiences. Eventually she meets the mimotaur itself, the masked woman who in the past has "ruled her acts."[36]

Every character and every incident in *Seduction* possess symbolic significance for Lillian's life. With a humorous note Nin calls the flamboyantly sexual figure of "Diana" Aphrodite. In one of the novel's most important scenes, the seductive Diana bathes nude in the ocean. She possesses Sabina's capacity to abandon herself to pleasure but is free from her compulsive appetite for conquest. Diana is more natural, and Lillian clearly admires her. Fred, "Christmas," gradually comes to represent Larry, the husband from whom Lillian is separated, a shy man who fears "the fiery core" of life that Lillian succeeds in reaching in Golconda. After Lillian has stumbled into a local con game by paying fifty dollars to release an American from jail, she is enlightened by a man called the "excavator." His real name is O'Connor; standing in for Doctor Hernandez, the excavator tells Lillian, " 'When you're so intent on freeing others you must be trying to free some part of yourself too.' " Gradually Lillian admits this. A journey within a journey, from

Golconda to San Luis, brings Lillian in contact with a family much
like her own (Hatcher's personality is similar to her father's); she
recalls having been lost as a child in the underground tunnels beneath their house. This is a terrifying memory that she manages to
exorcise through a lucid understanding of its inhibiting effect on
her life: *"When you choose to play in a realm far away from the
eyes of parents, you court death."*[37]

Lillian attends a festival in San Luis with the young Doctor
Palas. All this while, having made discoveries about herself in relation to her lovely, fastidious, lady-like mother, Lillian is preparing
to confess her sorrows and her hopes to Doctor Hernandez. But
she waits too long. When she returns to Golconda she discovers
that he has been killed by the drug smugglers. Her sorrow is the
deeper since she did not give him the intimate talk he sought from
her. Characteristically though, Anaïs Nin balances a loss with an
example of growth. She concludes Lillian's stay in Mexico with one
of the most limpid and rhythmically hypnotic of her prose passages, embedding in the words a tribute to Doctor Hernandez who
had commented that he did not know which drug Lillian needed,
"the one for forgetting or the one for remembering."[38]

The last part of *Seduction of the Minotaur* takes place on an
airplane and consists entirely of Lillian's recollections: first, of a
dazzling but frustrating evening when she, Doctor Hernandez,
Diana, Fred, and Edward visit the native dance halls of Golconda.
This scene brings together all the people of Golconda, the entire
community in the shared celebration of music and dance. Lillian's
desire to dance barefooted is opposed by Doctor Hernandez. But
since she desperately wants this physical contact with the earth, she
defies him. She rejects the clumsy Fred as a dancing partner with
a complaint that his boots hurt her feet. This scene brings Lillian
a rhapsodic vision. It is an experience of fusion that is comparable
to Djuna's immersion in the moonstorm. The gently humorous conclusion to this remembered evening takes place at Doctor Hernandez's "secret cove" where all but Fred bathe in the nude. (He is
afraid of Diana's sensuality.) Lillian experiences the promise of rebirth when she emerges from the water; she is now ready to accept

"her responsibility in the symbolic drama of [her] marriage." The rest of her return trip to the United States brings even more revelations about her past, carrying her back to relive the attic spankings by her father that caused her to associate pain with caresses and, consequently, to find Larry's totally loving treatment lacking in a "measure of pain;[39] back toward Jay to whose demands she had submitted, sacrificing her self until with the arrival of Sabina in their life, his abuses of Lillian's good nature became excessive; back, too, into the complicated threads of her own intense relationship with Sabina (the material of *Ladders to Fire*). Finally, Lillian completes her journey. She meditates upon the character of her husband, Larry. In an exuberant mood, she recognizes that the flatness he has shown her is self-protective. With a new sense of the possibility of complementarity in their marriage, she freely returns to it. Lillian is confident that since she has changed, the marriage will change as well.

These revelations of Larry occur in counterpoint against the rhythm of interspersed passages about travel to the moon. Again the theme of the double journey is emphasized. Lillian voyages into space, as Djuna did in "The Voice," at the same time that she burrows underground into the labyrinth of her past. The book's closing passage brings into fusion the images of space exploration and personal inner exploration. "In silence, in mystery, a human being was formed, was exploded, was struck by other passing bodies, was burned, was deserted. And then it was born in the molten love of the one who cared."[40]

Like *Seduction of the Minotaur* "The Voice" concludes with a splendid lyric passage, a description of the shape, the action of dream. It is a spiral, a "tower of layers without end," that ascends toward heaven, signifying aspiration and transcendence, while at the same time coiling downward into the lower regions, the personal hells of all who suffer. Besides providing reality with a complementary realm, dream serves as a metaphysical concept somewhat like Yeats' gyres, uniting polar zones, arising like a spiral which Nin describes as a vertical labyrinth or tower (another shape beloved by Yeats as well as the French Symbolists).

> The dream was composed like a tower of layers without end, rising upward and losing themselves in the infinite, or layers coiling downward, losing themselves in the bowels of the earth. When it swooped me into its undulations, the spiraling began, and this spiral was a labyrinth. There was no vault and no bottom, no walls and no return. But there were themes repeating themselves with exactitude.

Envisioned as a spiral-shaped tower, the dream unites realms that are ostensibly incapable of being brought into unity: the vast space above and the vast space below our earth, "l'azure" and "le gouffre," as they were called by the Symbolists. The one who dares to enter the dream must be able to endure solitude and must be strong enough to survive a series of explosions. In Nin's work, as in Hesse's, a disintegration of personality typically precedes a new alignment of elements into a new being:[41]

> If the walls of the dream seemed lined with moist silk, and the contours of the labyrinth lined with silence, still the steps of the dream were a series of explosions in which all the condemned fragments of myself burst into a mysterious and violent life, with the heavy maternal solicitude of the night ever attentive to their flowing.

The dream is the alembic in which a new self is ground into an explosive powder, fragments crushed, mixed with other fragments, then reassembled into a new combination of energies. This occurs at night, for darkness and silence are hospitable to magical adventures. What dares not grow in the harsh light of sun is encouraged to flower by the night's soft anonymity.

The rhapsody concludes with a metaphor that pictures the dream as an inspiration to movement, drawing us on in pursuit of its strange and lovely reverberations. Fulfilled, the dream is the unity of all that we know and can be, and these moments of fusion, of totality experienced, are the "eternal moments."

> The dream was synchronized. The miracle was accomplished. All the clocks chimed at midnight for the metamorphosis. It

was not time they chimed for, but the catching up, catching up with the dream. The dream was always running ahead of one. To catch up, to live for a moment in unison with it, that was the miracle. The life on the stage, the life of the legend dovetailed with the daylight, and out of this marriage sparked the great birds of divinity, the eternal moments.[42]

The spiral figure used by Nin to represent the dream is a subtle choice, for its sweeping movement has four dimensions: from right to left; left to right; upwards; and downwards. At the center from which arises the spiraling dream, is the self. Passing beyond this center in one direction there is confrontation with self—life. In a mood seeking consolation, Nin wrote, "But of course, I had the dream, this blessed drug [as an object of contemplation the spiral is thought to induce a state of ecstasy] . . . Only dreams did not calm my hunger because my dreams did not lead me away from life but towards it, always guiding me towards realization."[43] In the opposite direction, moving from the center to ascend the mystic "hole," one seeks transcendence; rising from the material world toward the realm beyond.

"I walk with dream unfurled," Nin has proclaimed.[44] And later, equally boldly: "I want to go on living the uncensored dream, the free unconscious." Ideals of total liberty—astonishing and admirable. But before they were fulfilled, Anaïs Nin had to immerse herself in the discovery of her own nature, first, as woman, later, as artist.

Rediscovering Woman

It is my thousand years of womanhood I am recording, a thousand women.

—*The Diary of Anaïs Nin, Volume VI*

Corresponding with his grown daughter Joaquin Nin once wrote, "Ma Grande Chérie: Your letter brought me one of the facets of your innumerable faces. An aspect of goodness and grace which reveals all the capacity for compassion of woman."[1] Using this sort of flattery he exhorts his daughter to be womanly: good, gracious, compassionate. In short, to be generous toward himself. Though enthralled by his image for many years, Anaïs Nin eventually freed herself from the ideal of woman which her father admired.

"The evolution of woman. I am living it and suffering it for all women."[2] One of the remarkable aspects of the adventure of Nin's life has been her determination to explore the nature of woman as fully as time and energy would permit. An even more dangerous ambition has been her desire to make of this exploration an assertion of her own multi-dimensionality. She has assumed one role after another, striving to feel at ease with a personal complexity that would frighten people less knowledgeable of psychology than she. Her confidence that rich personalities possess many aspects without disintegrating has given her the courage to experiment with herself. She has insisted that one role is not enough for a woman, particularly when this is a biologically determined role that covers but a third of her life span and makes no allowance for any but biological capabilities. Again and again Nin has proclaimed and has shown by her life that woman, like man, is complex and possesses the energy and the flexibility to play a variety of roles simultaneously. She can be friend, worker, creator, counselor, muse, lover, mother, wife, hostess, revolutionary, sage, scholar, and play still other roles without sacrificing precious contact with her authentic private self.

Individuation and multidimensionality have not been easy achievements for Anaïs Nin despite her positive attitude toward psychoanalysis and her willingness to seek its guidance whenever she felt she needed it. In *Diaries V* and *VI* she is still searching for certain qualities that are uniquely hers, not the result of someone else's influence on her. A study of the psychological obstacles impeding Nin's self-realization shows how tenacious a hold the ideal of mother has had on her. She became aware of the terrible power of this model or ideal very early in the course of her battle to become an individual and assertive self. In 1933 she wrote, "It is my maternal instinct which places me in danger."[3] The struggle is heroic for it is against an ideal that is unattainable without cruel personal sacrifice. Few societies wish woman to be more than mother. And fewer still actually assist her in achieving personal goals beyond or in addition to motherhood.

The Christian ideal of woman, worshipped and adored for centuries, is that of the Virgin Mary. Mary is a mother yet she is chaste. The supreme image of woman in the Western world combines two obviously irreconcilable conditions: virginity and motherhood. No woman can possibly live up to this ideal. If she tries to approximate its qualities, she will be self-sacrificing, submissive, merciful, and always sweet. She will have to learn to place the needs of others before her own. Of course she will have to renounce the desires of the body. The Roman Catholic Church most sternly enforces conformity to this ideal by forbidding sexual intercourse unless for the express purpose of reproduction; without forbidding sex, Protestantism nevertheless displays a long tradition of disapproval of sensual pleasure while Judaism despises and fears the female because of her shameful "primitive" connection with nature as evidenced by menstruation. These religions present uniformly a sus-picion of woman that is connected with her body and her sexuality; to overcome this suspicion, woman is draped with a cloak (literally, by Moslems) and hung with the trappings of an elevated moral na-ture arising supposedly from her superior capacity for compassion. Finally, she is commanded to live up to this bizarre combination of biological fecundity and physiological chastity. Man's persistent de-termination to deny abortion and to be the exclusive sexual partner of his wife, while allowing himself the privilege of many sexual partners, is proof that the sexuality of woman is still today unac-ceptable to many men and—what is worse—to many women. The availability of contraception for a few decades has not automatically revolutionized woman's role in society. She is still expected to be—first and foremost—a mother, even if she happens to possess a striking talent for some other type of work. The role of mother is, fundamentally, asexual.

So powerful an influence has the Christian ideal of woman had on Western culture that woman feels ennobled by her own sacri-fices and enriched by her own suffering. In *Diary II* Anaïs Nin voiced the common attitude that "to be violated is perhaps a need in woman, a secret erotic need."[4] When questioned about this many years later, she explained, "If someone with a will stronger than hers 'rapes' a woman, she is not responsible for the sexual act. These dreams may disappear when a woman is freed of guilt for her sexual desires."[5] Nin has attributed woman's masochism to her habit of self-denial in favor of gratifying the needs of her children: "I have a feeling that the masochism of woman is different from that of man. Hers comes from her maternal instinct. A mother . . . suffers, gives, feeds. A woman is taught not to think of herself, to be selfless, to serve, help. This masochism is almost natural to woman. She is brought up in it. (Example set in the family by my Spanish grandmother.) It is like the masochism of people brought up in the Catholic religion." At about the same time Nin complained: "I am embalmed because a nun leaned over me, enveloped me in her veils, kissed me. The chill curse of Christianity. I do not con-fess any more, I have no remorse, yet am I doing penance for my enjoyments? Nobody knows what a magnificent prey I was for Christian legends, because of my compassion and my tenderness for human beings. Today it divides me from enjoyment of life."[6]

Unless they are priests men do not demand chastity of themselves, nor do they labor under the burden of a superior capacity for self-sacrifice and self-denial in the service of others. When Joaquin Nin died, his room included only photographs of himself. When woman refuses man's demand for her indulgence, her compassion, even her forgiveness, she risks disappointing, even shocking him. When she insists upon sexual expression for herself, she risks his rejection. Divorce laws usually provide that the adulteress be denied custody of her children. Over and over again we see the intolerance of society for the woman who insists upon expressing several dimensions of herself at the same time. The good mother is not supposed to be a sexual being, except exclusively with her husband. The good mother is not a worker outside the home; inside the home she does not earn money because the work she does is not considered important enough to merit pay. She is not a creator, because if she is truly "feminine" she will prefer to sublimate her energies by participating in the work of some man. The good mother and the "womanly" woman are synonymous, and often anonymous. From life they ask nothing for themselves but the fulfillment that comes from being a part of the growth process of others. Nin's books trace her own and her characters' struggles against the mother in themselves, for whether it is her sexuality or her impulse toward work that is blocked, the woman must—in each case—bring out of her self a will toward individuation that is strong enough to counter the force of the internalized mother image. Near the end of *Seduction of the Minotaur* Lillian becomes aware that motherhood had prepared her for "abdicating" her self in a relationship with a demanding man.

"Birth" is the most naked account in Nin's writing of how procreation threatens the individual identity of the woman. A straightforward narrative of the delivery of a six-month stillborn female child, the "story" is a revision of the account of the actual event that occurs near the end of *Diary I*.[7] Although the piece is titled "Birth," the first sentence is the doctor's announcement that the baby is dead. Either the title is bitterly ironic, which would not be characteristic of Nin's tone, or someone besides the baby has been born. Actually it is the young woman who has "lost" the child who is herself born through this apparent sorrow. Speculating on her psychoanalysis with Otto Rank, Nin states: "The birth of the real me might have ended like that of my unborn child."[8] Near the close of "Winter of Artifice," she makes even more explicit the significance of the death of the six-month child: "The last time she had come out of the ether it was to look at her dead child, a little girl with long eyelashes and slender hands. She was dead. The little girl in her was dead too. The woman was saved."[9] The premature birth of the young woman as mother would have meant the death of other aspects of this woman; the fact that the child does not survive leaves her free to pursue her personal growth.

Nin's maturity demanded that she come to terms with her own yearning for a father, the same father who had—it seemed—abandoned her and her brothers. The child who died before being born symbolizes the infantile part of the author, the young woman who was unable to accomplish a true emotional reunion with her biological father. Her feelings about the loss of her baby were intimately connected with her sense of having been abandoned by her father. "I do not trust man as father," she wrote after the baby's death. "When I wished this child to die, it was because I felt it would experience the same lack [of a father]."[10] Although she feared the unreliability of man as father, Anaïs Nin deeply needed a relationship with a father-figure. The first cycle in her personal evolution is characterized by her repeated attempts to obtain "fathering" from an older man who would provide her with warmth, a sense of direction, and who would encourage her to write. These "fathers" were Henry Miller, René Allendy, Otto Rank, and—most important—her own father, Joaquin Nin. (Later, but fleetingly, Nin was tempted to accept ambiguous fathering from Edmund Wilson and, later still, Max Pfeffer.) The exquisite prose dance of "Winter of Artifice" portrays how the attempted union and equally necessary separation were accomplished by the intelligent, determined daughter who succeeded in healing the childhood wound inflicted by her father. This liberation is made the easier because the father is incapable of giving the genuine exchange of feeling the daughter longs for. Eventually she realizes that in losing this man as father, she has lost nothing but an image. Accepting this difficult truth, the daughter moves on to build her own life.

It was Otto Rank who helped Nin through the crucial transition from child or unformed dependent woman searching for a father into the more mature role of woman as mother. Nin's own break with her father seems to have become decisive in 1934 when she was working on "Winter of Artifice." Despite its limiting, even crippling aspects, the maternal role was for a time deeply gratifying to Nin. It enhanced her confidence in her femininity, while—presumably —allowing her to exorcise any guilt that followed the death of her baby. The role of mother gave Nin a comforting sense of security and control, for as the one who dispenses what others need—whether material things or love—the mother is in a position of power. Because she gives and because what she gives is desperately needed, she is certain of maintaining her value for others: "Rank began to show me how my concept of woman was *mother*. To protect, serve, mother, care for. So it was the mother in me which found uses for her talents, but the woman? It was being such a mother that made me feel I was a woman."[11]

The success with which Anaïs Nin made the transition from the role of child to the far more commanding one of mother may be seen, amusingly, in the changing nature of her relationships with two one-time father figures: Henry Miller and Rank himself. Nin's relationship with Miller brought her the connection with art and the artist's life that she associated with her father, yet Miller's appearance, values, and way of life were so directly opposite to her father's that her closeness to the American writer provided an enjoyable rebellion. A delight of undermining the patriarchal type of man appears in *Children of the Albatross* and is the basis of Anaïs Nin's attitude toward Edmund Wilson as described in *Diary IV*. Eventually, instead of the daughter eager to receive the wisdom of the older, more self-asured male, Anaïs Nin grew into the role of friend and benefactor to Miller. It became necessary, too, for her to free herself from an apparently ambiguous relationship with Otto Rank. Only ten months after she began treatment, Nin wrote: "I went to Rank to solve my conflict with my father, and only added another father to my life, and another loss."[12] As always, Nin's perception of her psychological situation was acute, but preceded her ability to change the situation complained of by reorganizing her energies. For a time Nin was so impressed by the brilliant Rank and by her therapy with him that she planned to become an analyst herself. In November of 1934 she went to New York to assist Rank with his patients. During this period she completed *House of Incest*. Not more than five months had passed, however, before she had rediscovered her authentic direction, writing. She gave up practicing analysis. After she left Rank, returning to Paris in 1935, Nin's need for a relationship with a wise older man seems to have been overcome.[13]

The novels of *Cities of the Interior* explore the conflicts of women who bring to their loves of men a maternal solicitude. With the important exception of Sabina, the women in the five novels offer their men the caring, the protectiveness, the generosity, the willingness to sacrifice themselves that describe the role of woman as mother. Because she is capable of this sort of lavish emotional generosity, the woman is well protected against the man's rejection. She has made him need her. But this security is won at a heavy price. It may threaten the woman with loss of self. In the relationships of fusion that Nin presents in her novels the partners must be well matched in strength of ego for the fusion to maintain itself. If one loses his or her self in the self of the other, there will not be fusion but a submersion and loss of one person's identity. "Mature people relate to each other without the need to merge," Nin wrote in *Diary IV*.[14] The danger of loss of self in a relationship is usually greater for the woman. Because she has been trained to subordinate herself to men, the attempt to merge or fuse with another may destroy her experience of herself as a self-sufficient person.

Lillian is the most conventionally maternal woman in Anaïs Nin's fiction. Her story spans *Cities of the Interior,* dominating the first and fifth novels in the group: *Ladders to Fire,* begun in 1937, and *Seduction of the Minotaur,* concluded in 1958. Separated from her husband Larry and her children (a part of Lillian's life that Nin does not describe), Lillian is living with a painter named Jay. Spontaneous, impetuous, somewhat unsure of her physical attractiveness, she is endowed with a winning but occasionally too forceful energy. The first part of *Ladders* is called "This Hunger"; Lillian is starved for love and for sexual passion. Because she believes she will be fulfilled with Jay, she has given up her piano in order to take a job that will support his ambition to paint. Jay repays her by having affairs with other women; since she has given up so much for him, Lillian resents this. Of course she also fears that she will be replaced. Having made Jay partially dependent, Lillian proceeds to disarm one of her rivals, Helen, by the same device: a cunningly directed maternalism. Lillian attempts to meet so many of Helen's needs that this woman will desire her continued friendship more than Jay's love-making. Ironically, Lillian strives to preserve a situation that is not really providing what she wants; her strategy is self-defeating too. By putting Jay's needs before her own, Lillian simply ensures her own deprivation by directing her energy away from her self. Naturally, her frustration and despair increase.

When Lillian becomes pregnant the reader gains an insight into her secret hopes. Talking to her unborn—never to be born—child, she laments: " 'You will not find on earth this father as large as the sky, big enough to hold your whole being and your fears larger than house or church. You will not find a father who will lull you and cover you with his greatness and his warmth. It would be better if you died inside of me, quietly in the warmth and in the darkness.' " What Lillian gives is what she secretly longs to receive, the affection, the sacrifice, the watchfulness, and love she has given Jay. Like most people who nourish such hopes, Lillian is disappointed. During the long party scene with which *Ladders* closes, Lillian commits "invisible hara-kiri"[15] with an outburst of self-criticism. The reader knows without being told explicitly that Lillian's relationship with Jay will soon end.

In *Seduction of the Minotaur,* a more mature and more relaxed

Lillian commits herself to a "journey homeward" toward her authentic self. This journey is circular, for it leads her back to her husband Larry, from whom she has been separated for some time. No longer offering men a mother's sacrificial love, the Lillian of *Seduction* is able to confront the "devastating discovery that she was not free,"[16] a necessary discovery if she is to move toward personal liberation through a series of experiences in Mexico that parallel specific wounding experiences of her childhood. Absorbed in this quest and intensely involved with her piano, Lillian does not seek erotic relationships with any of the novel's male characters. Like the loving but independent Renate of *Collages,* Lillian remains at a distance she herself defines, entering and withdrawing from friendships spontaneously. She is now able both to experience and to control her emotions without threat of going "crazy" and without fear of losing her sense of herself in an intense relationship with another person. One consequence of Lillian's new maturity and independence is her acceptance of the fatherly concern and guidance that Dr. Hernandez offers her. Earlier, in *Ladders to Fire,* Lillian had longed for a father to direct and protect her, but had been unable to accept such closeness lest she herself relapse into childish dependency. Dr. Hernandez is a male Ariadne. With his perceptive wisdom, Lillian is able to maneuver some of the more treacherous passages of her private labyrinth.

Lillian's Mexican quest brings her a series of new insights into her husband Larry. She learns to view him from a different perspective. Her tenderness for him is ignited once again; *Seduction* closes with Lillian's return home, presumably to resume her marriage. Dr. Hernandez has told her that "We live by a series of repetitions until the experience is solved, understood, liquidated . . ."[17] People are always changing in Nin's fictional world. Two who have once been close but have been separated by their individual paths of growth may come together again in a new state of fusion, refreshed by their period apart and strengthened by their newly gained wisdom. They love again.

Woman's attempt to offer man a mothering role is explored from two different perspectives in the novels that are focused on Djuna,

a woman who is a delight to others but a problem to herself. Lillian's confidante in *Ladders to Fire* and Sabina's in *A Spy in the
House of Love,* Djuna is complex: perceptive, wise, shy, tender,
fey, buoyant, and vulnerable. She is a dancer. And without being
aware of it, she is also rebellious and defiant, cleverly discovering
indirect ways to express her contempt of conventional, unimagina-
tive values. Repeatedly, Djuna chooses to become involved with
men who are in some way outside the norms of bourgeois masculinity: in *Children of the Albatross* they are gentle young men, bisexual or homosexual. In *The Four-Chambered Heart,* it is Rango,
a vagabond, part gypsy, a Marxist revolutionary, a man of violent
moods and little self-control, seemingly a wild and dangerous lover.

An important theme of *Children of the Albatross* is the friendship
of women with homosexual men. Djuna and her friends, Paul, Lawrence, Donald, and Michael, are whimsical, playful, tentative, and
elusive. They are attracted by experimentation. The children of the
albatross are "phosphorescent"; they are radiant. They give off the
light of their vital inner lives. They are sources of illumination and
revelation. While made luminous by their figurative father, the albatross, these children are weighed down by their biological fathers.
Self-righteous, sanctimonious, and pompous, these patriarchs are
shameless in the egotism with which they establish rules for everyone else. Even when the children escape, as they do in Nin's novel,
they must deal with the guilt that follows successful defiance. And
this guilt can be paralyzing. It can block fluidity, joy, spontaneity,
transcendent and beautiful forms of expression in art and sexuality
alike, prescribing instead conventional relationships of duty and
obligation.

Children of the Albatross traces a familiar theme of French literature, the initiation of a young man by an "older" woman. In her
late twenties, Djuna becomes fleetingly involved with Paul, seven-
teen; he is described as a "mist." The other "children" are young
homosexuals whose sexual preference indirectly expresses their rejection of the values taught by their families and teachers. The
"children" meet in Djuna's "house of innocence and faith."[18] Here
they dance, paint, and play, celebrating their love of freedom. The

young men and Djuna are drawn together by their fear of the tyrannical patriarch who thinks himself perfectly justified in denying
individual identity and autonomy to his daughters and his underage
sons. For Djuna this figure is symbolized by her memories of a cruel
and lecherous Watchman who terrified her when she was a child in
an orphanage. The need to create a counter-world in opposition to
the conventional patriarchal model ignites sympathy between the
rebellious "children," defiant women and gay young men, drawing
them together in friendship and sometimes in sex. Such friendships
and relationships, however, can easily become dangerous for the
woman, as Anaïs Nin's third and fourth published Diaries so clearly
reveal. Once again, "children," because they are dependent, take;
while "mothers," because they are empowered to provide what children need, give and give and give. Eventually they forget who they
are and what were their own desires.

From the start it is clear to the reader of *Children of the Albatross* that Djuna's relationship with Paul will be brief and will provide little emotional sustenance for her besides the thrill of participating in a young man's defiance of his father. Of course Paul's
family disapproves of Djuna not only because she is "older," but
also because of her profession as a dancer. A description of a
"sealed room" in Djuna's lovely house suggests that she has not yet
experienced her full potential, her self; if she had, she would choose
different men. Moreover, her dream of herself as Ariadne clearly
prophesies that after she has guided Paul safely through his personal labyrinth, she will be abandoned. Indeed, Paul embarks on an
exciting journey to India, leaving Djuna behind. She is unable to
console herself with the friendship of Michael and Donald, and her
mood of emptiness and dissatisfaction with herself provokes her to
look deeper into her own unexplored "cities," even to consider
whether the forceful, even crude masculinity of a man like Jay
might shock her into seeking a fuller emotional life.

It is not Jay though but Rango, a guitar player and communist,
who becomes Djuna's lover in the next, more mature phase of her
development. While richer and more satisfying than her relationship
with Paul, the love of Djuna and Rango is profoundly frustrating,

and its incisive and wonderfully penetrating presentation in *The Four-Chambered Heart* exposes the way in which woman is trapped by her need to give the appearance of "goodness" and by the guilt that prevents her from living as she wishes. A grey book, its dominant mood heavy in contrast to the lightness and luminosity of *Children, The Four-Chambered Heart* brings together lovers who are weighted down to the point of exhaustion by obligations to demanding hypochondriacs: Rango to his wife Zora; Djuna to her father. The lovers console each other at night on their houseboat which is moored in the Seine. Heavy rains force Rango and Djuna to move up and down the river. Like their relationship, their houseboat does not go any place; it merely plies its way back and forth over the same area. The terrifying phantom of the Watchman from Djuna's childhood becomes real in the person of a drunk who spies on the lovers and threatens Djuna until Rango frightens him away.

Love reaches its peak in the first thirty pages of the novel. After that, there is conflict and violence, a futile attempt on Djuna's part to break the relationship by escaping to England. A night of terror arrives. Zora tries to murder Djuna. Filled with his own despair, Rango comes to the boat very late and falls into a depressed sleep. And Djuna—now desperate to initiate change of some sort—begins to tear up the floor boards. She is determined to let the barge sink if it will, herself and Rango along with it. Her action brings on the long-needed motion. The houseboat is torn loose from its mooring and is swept down the river. It does not sink. At the end of the novel a fisherman brings a drenched doll out of the water with a joke about its having tried to commit suicide. Closing with the sentence "Noah's ark had survived the flood,"[19] *The Four-Chambered Heart* affirms the ideal of the couple but stresses the need for this particular couple to part. The suffering, emotionally paralyzed Djuna has drowned, so says the lifeless image of the doll. But she has a chance to be reborn.

The pattern that Rango, Djuna, and Zora lived is related not only to the ancient love triangle and the drama of jealousy, but more profoundly to the competition of daughter and mother for the devotion of the father. Because of her guilt Djuna panders to Zora's outrageous demands: her hysterically induced illnesses; her obsessions; and tolerates the other woman's lack of common sense and her miserliness. Djuna gives Zora her own clothing and makes other sacrifices in order to buy medicine for her lover's wife. Guilty together, Djuna and Rango try to compensate Zora for the loss of his sexual love (ironically, she has rejected this years earlier). As the "little mother," Djuna ministers to the woman whose man she imagines she has stolen, while Rango, too, is gratified by serving Zora whose neurotic illness enables other people to feel superior to her while at the same time flattering images of themselves as "good." Djuna's situation is classically "feminine." To the image of herself as warm, charitable, modest, and loving, she has sacrificed the deep needs of her individuality. The real woman has become an image of conventional femininity, a doll.

The Four-Chambered Heart ruthlessly exposes the sources of woman's "goodness." Her assumption of moral superiority is shown to be a shield, a strategy employed for self-aggrandizement and self-protection. Worse still, the woman who insists on placing her goodness at the center of her relationship splits herself irrevocably. The mother-type is tender, reliable, gentle, a protector and nourisher of life. She suffers. And she sometimes experiences conflict between love and sexuality. In Nin's writings the sexual woman is represented by Sabina, an important presence since *House of Incest,* which was first published in 1936.

In *House of Incest* Nin depicted—and with unmistakable agony—the split in modern woman which has divided her into parts, the body cut off from the emotions. The "I" of *House* struggles to attain a sense of union with her body, her sensuality and sexuality. Self-aware, responsible, the "I" is capable of love but cannot express her sexuality. The book's two other women personify ways of relating to erotic and sexual possibilities that attract the "I." One is Sabina, a powerfully sexual woman. "When I saw you, Sabina," the narrator declares, "I chose my body." Sabina's voice is "rusty with the sound of curses and the hoarse cries that issue from the delta in the last paroxysm of orgasm." She is mysterious and haunting: "Her black cape hung like black hair from her shoulders, half-draped,

half-floating around her body."[20] Sabina is a portrait of woman as
witch, as the dangerous seductress in flowing black. Spontaneous,
sensuous, apparently totally free to enjoy sexuality without restraint,
Sabina is marvelously appealing to the narrator, who longs to slip
inside the other woman's body. And yet there is conflict; the narrator knows that Sabina is incapable of love.

The "I" of House of Incest is also attracted by the representation
of Jeanne, who is associated with the intense, insular, "incestuous"
loves of the sort that Nin has explored in some of the pieces collected in *Under a Glass Bell,* as well as in "Winter of Artifice" and
Children of the Albatross. Jeanne loves her brother, the male image
of herself. This love is no more substantial than a shadow: "When
my brother sat in the sun and his face was shadowed on the back of
the chair, I kissed his shadow. Our love of each other is like one
long shadow kissing, without hope of reality."[21]

Paralyzed by conflict, the "I" of *House of Incest* is strongly
drawn to the attitudes toward love represented by these contrasting
figures: toward the spontaneous seizing of any desire, on the one
hand; on the other, toward the alluring, forbidden love of her
brother, a sterile but safe love. In order to resist both dangers, the
one infantile, the other perverse, the "I" must embark upon a
journey into the house of incest. Jeanne is her guide: "The rooms
were chained together by steps. . . . The windows gave out on a
static sea, where immobile fishes had been glued to painted back-
grounds. Everything had been made to stand still in the house of
incest, because they all had such a fear of movement and warmth,
such a fear that all love and all life should flow out of reach and be
lost!"

Lot is discovered caressing his daughter's breast. There is a
white plaster forest, a "forest of decapitated trees, women carved
out of bamboo, flesh slatted like that of slaves in joyless slavery,
faces cut in two by the sculptor's knife, showing two sides forever
separate, eternally two-faced, and it was I who had to shift about
to behold the entire woman."[22]

This image of woman as stiff and joyless, unable to move or to
live, is a terrifying vision of modern woman, whose physical pas-

sions have been denied as irreconcilable with the ideals of chastity, goodness, and sweetness that civilized man wishes her to embody. The Virgin Mary, the supreme symbol of motherhood, is sweet and sexless. But Anaïs Nin does not end *House of Incest* with such a hopeless image. The final, seventh part of the work is a meditation by the author on her book and how writing it helped her confront her personal illness. "I walked into my own book, seeking peace . . . and I bruised myself against my madness." This terrifying descent into illness is healing, however, for it serves to exorcise the visions both of Sabina and Jeanne. The "I" now proposes a new image of woman, a dancer who at first dances "the dance of the woman without arms." She confesses that her arms were taken away from her as a punishment for clinging. "I clung. I clutched all those I loved; I clutched at the lovely moments of life; my hands closed upon every full hour . . . And I strained and I held so much that they broke; they broke away from me. Everything eluded me then. I was condemned not to hold."[23]

Sabina continues to occupy a prominent place in Nin's later fiction. Both Lillian and Djuna are fascinated by Sabina's sexuality; they are infatuated with her and envy her dramatic display of freedom. *Ladders to Fire* presents an exploration of two women's desire for fusion in a relationship with each other. When Sabina appears in Jay's life, Lillian is terribly threatened. Having disposed of an earlier rival, Helen, by overwhelming her with friendship, Lillian attempts to repeat this strategy with Sabina. An interesting complication arises when she discovers that she herself is strongly attracted to Sabina. Since they are opposites, the two women seek to merge in order to complete themselves by absorbing strengths and capacities each lacks. Furthermore, both are angry at the man, Jay. Although he and Sabina are attracted to each other, they are natural enemies because both are Don Juan types, seeking to express freedom through sexual conquest. For her part, Lillian is angry at Jay because on a deep level he ignores her, annihilates her being by failing to take seriously her needs and desires. Jay, who has dominated Lillian, would like to dominate Sabina. But the women ally against him, expressing their rebellion through dance. To taunt the men, they deliberately dance together erotically in a workingclass tavern. The men react by throwing the women out. Intoxicated by their display of independence, the two women go to Sabina's room and lie down together. But then they discover that sexual union is not what they seek in each other:

> Not this the possession they imagined. No bodies touching would answer this mysterious craving in them to become each other. Not to take, but to imbibe, absorb, change themselves. Sabina carried a part of Lillian's being, Lillian a part of Sabina, but they could not be exchanged through an embrace. It was not that. Their bodies touched and then fell away, as if both of them had touched a mirror, their own image upon a mirror. They had felt the cold wall, they had felt the mirror that never appeared when they were taken by a man. Sabina had merely touched her own youth, and Lillian her free passions.[24]

Their longing for fuller, more developed, and more powerful selves has led Lillian and Sabina into an embrace from which both withdraw.

Djuna, too, is fascinated by Sabina. To her, Djuna attributes the unexpressed sexuality of all women: "Sabina is only behaving as all women do in their dreams, at night. . . . In my dreams I have been Sabina. I have escaped from your [Rango's] tormenting love, caressed all the interchangeable lovers of the world. Sabina cannot be made alone responsible for acting the dreams of many women, just because the others sit back and participate with a secret part of their selves. Through secret and small vibrations of the flesh they admit being silent accomplices to Sabina's acts. At night we have all tossed with fever and desire for strangers."[25]

Djuna suffers because she does not dare seize the freedom to love "strangers," a freedom that Sabina enjoys and inadvertently expresses for the other women in Nin's books. Yet Djuna is caught in the trap of awareness, for like the "I" of *House of Incest,* she recognizes (or rationalizes) that the liberty to enjoy a variety of sexual partners seems to be in conflict with the commitment required by a deep relationship. In posing this dilemma, Nin goes beyond questions about woman's sexuality to probe the vast and very troublesome area of how individual sexual fulfillment can be reconciled with the human need for devotion, loyalty, and stability in a union of two.[26]

Ironically, Sabina is no more in possession of a strongly unified self than are the women who long to be like her. In *A Spy in the House of Love* she is compelled to confront herself as a transparent, multilayered woman who conceals her emptiness beneath a swirling cape. Attempting to imitate man's capacity to enjoy sexual experiences with strangers, Sabina enters erotic adventures with different men. She is fortunate in having a husband who cares deeply for her and either does not see or pretends not to be aware of her relationships with others. It is, however, partly this "fathering" that leaves her dissatisfied with Alan, feeding her need for others.

After a brief opening in which the lie detector responds to Sabina's phone call by agreeing to pursue the guilty "spy," the structure of the novel suggests a downward spiraling shape, a motion of deflation and dejection. Sabina encounters a series of men with whom she has unsatisfactory relationships. Each is more disappointing than its predecessor. First, an unnamed man (perhaps he is Philip) with whom she has a rendezvous only a few blocks from her own apartment where her husband Alan waits, believing her to be appearing in a play in another state. Philip, who evokes all the gay charm of "Vienna before the war," is a handsome opera star. He is a Don Juan, and Sabina, fearing to be conquered, is unable to attain sexual pleasure with him. She pursues Mambo, a black political exile, temporarily a drummer with a Greenwich Village music group. But this man is aware that Sabina enjoys his ostensible "primitivism," and he withdraws from her in a mood of humiliated pride. On Long Island she meets John, a former aviator. Seemingly close to insanity, John flees from Sabina after a single sexual experience. Next, Sabina becomes involved with Donald, a homosexual, who loves her in a tender way that awakens her maternal nature. As she moves from one of these men to another, Sabina's despair increases.

A reunion with Jay abruptly halts this series of encounters. An ironic double unveiling takes place. Sabina's fluidity and air of mystery have always iritated Jay. Some years earlier they had had "ravenous" intercourse in a rapidly ascending and descending elevator. "At that moment Sabina had been stripped of all mystery and Jay had tasted what the mystery contained: the most ardent frenzy of desire." Consequently, he has painted her as "a mandrake with fleshly roots, bearing a solitary purple flower in a bell-shaped corolla of narcotic flesh."[27] To Jay, Sabina is flesh exclusively, erotic passion, "ravenous" (Lillian too suffers from "this hunger").

But Sabina is far more complex than Jay imagines her to be, more complex and yet emptier. In Duchamp's "Nude Descending a Staircase," Sabina discovers a wholly different metaphor for her self. "Eight or ten outlines of the same woman, like many multiple exposures of a woman's personality, neatly divided into many layers, walking down the stairs in union." There are many Sabinas superimposed one upon another. Defensively, she asks: "Was this the crime to have sought to marry each Sabina to another mate, to match each one in turn by a different life?"[28] Sabina has no center; otherwise her personality would not fall apart as it does at the novel's end. Her guilt is caused by her irresponsibility; she has tried to live like the most rapacious of men, the Don Juan who pursues, takes, enjoys, and abandons. Sabina resembles Anaïs Nin's father, in fact, and her attempt to live by adventure and conquest brings destruction to others and misery to herself. Nonetheless, her psychic collapse at the end of *Spy* provides an opportunity for renewal, for she has been brave enough to confront her own basic hollowness. Lillian in *Ladders to Fire* is self-less but for a different reason; she has given away too much of her self; Sabina, who seems to have many selves, is also self-less because she is too frightened to live from the deep core or center of her self. She gives nothing; consequently, she is the least "feminine" though the most sexual of Anaïs Nin's women characters. This is why she is an imposter, a "spy" in the house of love.

The way in which woman's nature has been reduced, simplified, and, finally, split into parts is deeply probed in Nin's writings. Most fascinating are her insights into the dangers to the woman in a relationship of intense love or fusion. The gentle, generous woman is likely to be received with attention and admiration, the more so if she returns to her friends and lovers flattering images of themselves. The danger though is that soon she may be overwhelmed by their demands to the point of losing touch with herself. In fusion, identification with the other depends upon the anticipation of his needs. The one who seeks to gratify these needs enacts two parts, intuitively placing himself within the feeling range of the other while simultaneously playing the visible and articulate role one is expected by that other person to play. The art of empathy is dangerous because the needs of the self are so easily confused with those of the other. They can be lost sight of altogether.

When the boundaries between the self and others are maintained, playing a part in their quest for identity can be exhilarating and gratifying: "I am like the crystal in which people find their mystic unity," Nin wrote in 1936:[29] But when the self is overwhelmed by the expectations of others and by the obligation to fulfill them, shattering can result. When Rank asked Anaïs Nin, " 'What brought you here?' " she replied, " 'I felt like a shattered mirror.' "[30] Woman's identification with a mirror also appealed to Virginia Woolf, who wittily wrote, "Women have served all these centuries as looking glasses possessing the magic and delicious power of reflecting the figure of man at twice its natural size."[31] Were it not for the pleasure reflected back to the giver of a flattering image, women would probably have refused to function as mirrors or crystals centuries ago. Creating the conditions in which others are able to be and feel their best is perhaps one of the most satisfying rewards of conventional femininity. It is basic both to woman's relationship with man and to all of her mothering and nurturing activities. It can also, as Nin complained, kill her.

This fear that mothering can kill the one who devotes her life to it is expressed with a mixture of pathos and wry humor in the fifth *Diary*. Nin dreams that her mother, now dead, did not die of natural causes but took her own life because of the destructive monotony of filling endless lunch boxes. " 'Everyday more lunch boxes. Lunch boxes again. Nothing but lunch boxes.' The implication to me was that my mother had filled too many lunch boxes and had finally gone mad and committed suicide."[32] During the years spanned by the first four Diaries, Nin's own mother is rarely mentioned, for the author was devoting tremendous energy to escaping the role represented in her life by Rosa Culmell. Nin tells us in *Diary I* that she adored her mother until at the age of sixteen she repudiated Catholicism: "I gave myself totally and annihilatingly to my mother. For years I was lost in my love of her."[33] With the rebellion against the life she saw her mother living and suffering came the rejection of Catholicism as a source of this role. The combined distance of time and experience gradually healed Nin's sense of estrangement from her puritanical and pious mother. As she worked in analysis with Inge Bogner, the author became able to accept her own maternal qualities as positive and generous inheritances from her own mother. In a touching manner *Diary V* portrays Anaïs Nin's attempts to seek inner reconciliation as she and her brother Joaquin sort through Rosa Culmell's belongings after her death.

However, before this compassionate spirit of maturity was achieved, Anaïs Nin had to suffer her own agonies of nourishing, to flounder and to sink, nearly to drown, in a sea of demands from those whom she encouraged to need her. Her fiercest protests against compulsive mothering appear in *Diary III*. In *Diary II* she began to refer to her "children": Jean Carteret, Conrad Moricand, Gonzalo and Helba, and Henry Miller. To these were added between 1939 and 1944 the poets John Dudley and Robert Duncan, Kenneth Patchen (off and on), Pierce Harwell, an astrologer, the actress Luise Rainer, and, still, Henry Miller. When Nin extended her generosity to John Dudley, she wrote: "The mother of artists has given birth again." But she was struggling to free herself from these entanglements. After having received requests for money from both Robert Duncan and Henry Miller, Nin proclaimed: "I believe the maternal in me, the mother, has been properly devoured, to the last bit, and she is dead."[34]

Time was yet to pass before this prophecy materialized and

Anaïs Nin was to develop control over her powerful impulse to share everything she possessed with people designated as "children." Her grief at having been compelled to put Robert Duncan at a distance reveals the sorrow she experienced in the struggle to gratify her maternal desire without sacrificing her personal aspiration to be a creator. Although she tried, Nin did not shed her burdens quickly enough to save herself. In the winter of 1942 she experienced a sudden sense of emotional depletion. "I don't know what day I felt: *No puedo más* (I can't bear any more). But it came with such violence that I broke down. First came an extreme weakness, so extreme I could not climb the stairs to my home. I had to take them like mountain climbing, resting between each step. Then came the weeping. Uncontrollable weeping. It seemed to me that I was broken for good, physically and spiritually."[35] She entered psychotherapy with a Jungian called Martha Jaeger. This doctor did much to help Anaïs Nin develop an expanded concept of woman.

The essential concept in this development was a redefinition of the idea of mother and, by implication, of woman. Besides the ideas of Martha Jaeger, two of M. Esther Harding's books were the primary influence on Nin's thinking about woman. In 1935 she read *The Way of All Women* for the first time (she returned to it in 1946). Like Jaeger, Harding was a follower of Jung and in this book and the even more impressive *Woman's Mysteries Ancient and Modern,* she uses the evidence of art, archaology, and mythology to argue for the validity of a concept of woman that is far older and far richer than that promoted by Christianity. Harding shows how the archetype of mother is related to the many moon goddesses that were worshipped in the ancient world. In primitive tribes "the moon is in fact the First Woman whose influence on men is invariably evil," explains Harding. The goddesses of the moon (Diana, or Artemis, Ishtar, Hecate, Shakti, and the Celtic Anu or Annis) were the givers of life and the protectors of fertility, but they were also attributed with the destructive powers of nature (particularly floods). The female supreme deity was "dual in her very nature. She lived her life in phases, manifesting the qualities of each phase in turn. In the upper-world phase, corresponding to the bright moon, she is good, kind, and beneficent. In the other phase, corresponding to the time when the moon is dark, she is cruel, destructive, and evil."[36]

The recovery of woman's complexity, which Jungian thought makes possible, has been immensely valuable to Anaïs Nin. The ancient relationship of woman to the moon serves to restore or bring back into the open two aspects of feminine nature which Judaism and Christianity have condemned and attempted to repress: her destructive power and her sexuality. Anthropologists and other scholars now know that the idea of a "virgin" goddess did not originally indicate a sexual condition but a social and psychological one. A "virgin" was—simply—unmarried. As Harding reminds us, the Moon Mother was "goddess of sexual love but not of marriage." Her priestesses, and in some societies all women, performed sexual acts with strangers in the temples that were devoted to the goddesses of the moon. The Virgin Ishtar, for example, was also addressed as "The Prostitute." "The word 'virgin' itself has not, strictly speaking, the meaning which we attach to it; the correct Latin expression for the untouched virgin is not 'virgo,' but 'virgo intacta.' " In short, "a girl belongs to *herself* while she is virgin— unwed— and may not be compelled either to maintain chastity or to yield to an unwanted embrace."[37] The impact of patriarchal Judaism and Christianity on these ancient concepts is too clear to require comment.

Anaïs Nin's discovery of this older ideal of woman had rich consequences, as well it might, for it enabled her to conceptualize a fuller, more complex idea of woman than that she inherited from Spanish Catholicism. As mother, woman is endowed with tremendous powers of destruction, something Nin had longed for ever since she met Henry Miller and grew to be in awe of his straightforward devotion to writing. This devotion enabled him to deny or set aside the needs of others whenever they interfered with his own plans for his time and other resources. June, too, was willing or able to harm others in pursuit of her own needs. This is what Nin could not do. Her yearning to do it did not mean that she wished to express selfishness and other harmful impulses, but that she desperately needed to escape from the many burdens she had assumed in a spirit of womanly compassion. The choice of how to use one's destructive energies is one that woman has as much right to make as man. Ultimately, in fact much later, when Nin had gained a sure sense of her identity as an artist, she began to present in writing and lectures a highly ethical view: that all people have a responsibility to recognize and then to transform their negative emotions into positive actions.

Once again we return to the question of woman's sexuality and man's and woman's mutual need for relationships of tenderness and passion. The Jungian view of woman is expansive; it allows of many dimensions so that sexuality, independence, and mothering are not mutually exclusive, as in the Christian view. Through the ages woman has accepted man's need for multiple relationships while man has clung to the idea that women are "above" sexual desires or more easily able to repress them than themselves, or able to experience their sexuality only when "in love." That these ideas are false has now been conclusively shown by recent research into the physiology of female sexuality. Social changes and new discoveries force us to ask questions about the future nature of relationships between men and women. Now that woman has the power to decline motherhood she can enjoy as many life choices as man now enjoys. And if she is to become economically and emotionally self-sustaining, who is to say whether she will find marriage as attractive as women of the past? Independent women, like independent men, will have greater opportunities to choose their partners freely and to meet, if they wish, the challenge of maintaining multiple relationships.

Since Anaïs Nin has devoted so great a part of her writing to exploring woman's nature, her view of the future is bound to be a perceptive and valuable one. In an interview conducted in 1972 she expressed the following ideas in response to a question about love:

Q. You have written that "the tragic aspect of love appears only when one tries to fit a boundless love into a limited one. All around me I find that one love is not enough, two is not

enough. The women I know seek to add one love to another."
Can this need "to add one love to another" be reconciled with
legal marriage?

A. I believe in a few years we will dispense with the legal
marriage. Marriage and divorce should not be in the power of
the law or lawyers. Society will have to recognize all children
as equal, legitimate or illegitimate. And marriage should be
merely a free choice of the one at the center of one's life. The
idea of multiple relationship has always been granted to man.
It will have to be granted to woman.[38]

Rarely does Anaïs Nin receive credit for her daring social views
or for writing about areas of experience that have previously been
forbidden to women by force of public opinion.[39] Her predecessor,
the absolute mistress of the realm of eroticism and love, is Colette.
Both Nin and Colette have been considered scandalous as women
and as writers. Both are brilliant psychologists of love. And both
have had the courage to write about what they know. Of the two,
Nin is the more consistently "feminine"; she has not, as did Colette,
written about love, sensuality, and sexuality from the point of view
of the male. In their writing both women have explored homoeroti-
cism and homosexuality (male and female); the friendships between
homosexual men and heterosexual women; love between the older
woman and the younger man; adultery; the psychic complications
of the love triangle; and the grief and anger of the woman who,
aroused, fails to achieve orgasm. Besides the topics that she shares
with Colette, Nin has written of fantasized incest (see especially
"Winter of Artifice"); of onanism ("The Voice"); of the white
woman's sexual exploitation of the black man *(Spy)*; of fellatio
(Collages); and, most notoriously, of the female Don Juan. The
last topic has never, as far as I know, been explored in the serious
literature of England or the U.S. It is not surprising that *A Spy in
the House of Love* was turned down by 127 publishers or that this
book, once printed at Nin's own expense, met with misunderstanding and condemnation (even from women).

The ambience of Nin's fiction is always sensuous. She excels, as does Colette, at evoking a seductive physical world, an abundance of tantalizing sounds, aromas, and colors, invitations to the senses. Often, the sensuous atmosphere turns toward the sensual and sometimes toward the erotic. The most intensely erotic of Nin's books remains the early *House of Incest,* in which the tension between desire and frustration is almost excruciating. This book sets the pattern for Nin's later novels. There is the sensuous atmosphere. There is always an invitation to experience the pleasures of the body. There is excitation; there is erotic allure. But there is rarely a sustained sexual encounter. The longest sexually fulfilled love is that of Djuna and Rango, and even this is short-lived because it is based upon a neurotic entanglement of three. All of Nin's women characters experience conflict between their sense of responsibility toward others and the impulse to seize pleasure. Even Sabina suffers, not because her ideal of sexual experience without emotional commitment is wrong, but because she is *unconsciously* convinced that it is wrong. Nin has written, "I see Sabina as a portrait of modern woman, seeking to break taboos but still a prey to guilt."[40] The three women, Lillian, Djuna, and Sabina, never cease to struggle. They are always striving to attain the ideal state of emotional and sexual synthesis.

Although Anaïs Nin has defended the right of woman to maintain the multiple relationships that have been man's privilege through the centuries, she does ultimately reaffirm a faith in heterosexuality and in the couple. Taken together, her statements about gender, sexuality, and eroticism reveal a recognition and a conviction that individuals have different capacities and needs and that society must provide opportunities for fulfillment without censure. This is particularly important for woman, whose sexuality has been so severely restricted by the written and unwritten laws of the past. As woman's concept of her identity expands and her self-confidence grows, she experiences expansion of her erotic nature along with a belief in her right to express this nature. As in her views of the self, of time, space, and reality, Nin is—in the area of eroticism—a relativist. The clearest expression of her ideas is found in an essay of 1974:

The true liberation of eroticism lies in accepting the fact that there are a million facets to it, a million forms of eroticism, a million objects of it, situations, atmospheres, and variations. We have, first of all, to dispense with guilt concerning its expansion, then remain open to its surprises, varied expressions, and (to add my personal formula for the full enjoyment of it) fuse it with individual love and passion for a particular human being, mingle it with dreams, fantasies, and emotion for it to attain its highest potency. . . . the stronger the passion is for one individual, the more concentrated, intensified, and ecstatic the ritual of one to one can prove to be.[41]

Transforming the Muse

Moira spreads the vast cardboard trays with rosy sea shells, pearls, beads, pins, small mirrors, and with glue we turn them into fantasy earrings and pins. On a large table she also designs textiles. Her black hair curls around her forehead, around her ears in small ringlets, she looks like a harem woman, her eyes dark and glistening, but she is another one of tomorrow's women.

—*The Diary of Anaïs Nin, Volume III*

Among the most original aspects of Anaïs Nin's writing is her candid revelation of the psychological obstacles woman must overcome when she defines herself as artist, and among the most valuable are the descriptions of her four periods of psychoanalysis. Except for Doris Lessing and May Sarton, women novelists have not drawn full or detailed portraits of themselves in their fiction. In this respect, *The Golden Notebook* and Nin's *Diaries* are rich subjects for comparison.[1] Generally, although for different reasons, psychologists too have ignored the woman creator. One of the themes of Nin's *Diary* is the story, perhaps never before told, how woman, trained to exert all her efforts toward pleasing others, to serve and even to obey, can redirect her energy toward defining herself as an artist. One dimension of this important theme is Nin's disclosure of the role of psychoanalysis in her transformation of herself from muse to creator. She tells us that without repeated periods of psychoanalysis she might never have written her novels or dared to publish her Diary.

Stated in the most basic terms, Nin's problem demanded that she balance exaggerated motherliness with qualities that she refers to as "destructive," but that—on close observation—seem to require not so much harming others as denying their claims to her time and affection. Encouraged to do so by Otto Rank, Nin interpreted this as a problem of gender; men were capable of creation because they were capable of destruction. Consequently, she longed to develop her own potential for "destructive" acts, and for a time formed intense relationships with people whose supposed destructiveness she admired: for example, June and Henry Miller and Gonzalo More. To become an artist, then, meant developing the power of destruction in herself, and that required relinquishing part of her feminine identity, as expressed in nurturing, in order to assume the "masculine" capacity of putting work before personal relationships. This, of course, was very difficult to do. At the same time another obstacle appeared in the form of a question about woman's essential nature. A study of the images prominent in folklore and literature shows woman as possessing a "dark" side: a mysterious, irrational, impulsive, perfectly destructive side represented by the figures of *femme fatale,* witch, siren, or the moon goddesses like Ishtar and Hecate.

The discovery that woman like man might possess a capacity for destruction was presented in the complex tale of "Hedja," a story that reverberates with its author's temporary anxiety about what woman may actually be like when stripped of her Islamic veils and Christian cloak of saintliness. "Hedja" allegorizes the evolution of a woman painter from her "natural" primitive condition through her veiling, or "civilizing," by man; it concludes with this woman's rejection of veils as she asserts her naked being. The child Hedja is cruel. Her "greatest pleasure consisted in inserting her fingers inside pregnant hens and breaking the eggs, or filling frogs with gasoline and setting a lighted match to them."[2] While helping a friend lighten her skin, Hedja brutally rubs the child's forehead raw with a stone. Hedja enjoys causing pain. Pain seems natural to her because of the female's instinctive relation to the suffering of birth and death. Primitive people accepted the double nature of woman in her relationship to the moon with its changing phases. "The Moon Goddess was thus giver of life and of all that promotes fertility, and at the same time she was the wielder of the destructive powers of nature. To the ancients her contradictory character was an essential factor, frankly recognized. But viewed from our rational and causal standpoint a deity can be either friendly or malicious but cannot be both. For God is conceived of as good: evil is always the work of the devil."[3]

Civilization, especially Judaic-Christian civilization, has developed as a result of man's conquest of the natural world and therefore of woman, who is believed to be closer to this realm than he. Man has been determined to deny or to repress woman's intimate connection to instinctual and sometimes violent life processes; modern man does not accept the dual nature of woman that in ancient times endowed her with power and wholeness. Man "veiled" woman in order to conceal from her and from himself this power. Then, as Otto Rank admits in "Feminine Psychology and Masculine Ideology," man redefined woman to suit his own needs. Rank finds this to be the meaning of Adam's creation of Eve, after the first woman, Lilith, who sprang from the same source as Adam, was rejected by him. "This strange story of the first woman, Lilith, neglected in favor of her more popular competitor, Eve, also implies the existence of two types of woman: the weak, dependent, childlike woman who all her life remains, so to speak, a daughter, and the independent, strong woman of prefamilial matriarchal organization who draws her strength and self-reliance from motherhood. Of this latter woman, or rather, of this force in woman, man always was and still is afraid, because it symbolizes the epitome of irrationality, the marvel of creation itself."[4] The Eve type is a castrated woman, in a sense, for she has been cut off from her "dark," irrational nature. This mutilation is exactly the split that Nin projected with such grief and agony in *House of Incest*. Heavily veiled, so that her body, her sensuality could not be seen, woman became a mystery, a puzzle to herself but a lure to man. In *The Novel of the Future* Nin comments: "The man who has made the definitive conquest of nature, the American man, is the one most afraid of *woman as nature,* of the feminine in himself."[5] Simone De Beauvoir in *The Second Sex* discusses at length man's projection of everything he does not understand, the irrational, onto the figure of woman. Regardless of who she might actually be as an individual, the woman becomes "the other." To man she represents a mystery, a possible danger, an invitation to conquest; he wants to tame her, to civilize her along with the rest of the natural world.

At first as the Hedja of Nin's story begins to shed her literal veils, the veils of Islam, she moves further and further from the reality of primitive woman. First, she leaves the East for France where she adopts Western dress. Though outwardly a modern woman, Hedja remains elusive, ambiguous, mysterious: "Her speech revealed and opened no doors. It was labyrinthian." Restrained and delicate, self-effacing and self-sacrificing, Hedja "concealed her voraciousness and her appetites." Hedja's surface of perfect femininity attracts a Romanian artist named Molnar. They marry. At once Molnar begins to turn his exotic wife into a lady; he wants to make her conform to the Christian ideal of the Blessed Virgin Mary, "Our Lady." In this "second veiling" Hedja is disguised as a genteel, middle-class woman. "At every turn nature must be subjugated. Very soon, with his coldness, he represses her violence. Very soon he polishes her language, her manners, her impulses. He reduces and limits her hospitality, her friendliness, her desire for expansion."[6]

The civilizing of Hedja greatly benefits Molnar. Like Lillian in Nin's novel *Ladders to Fire,* Hedja gives up her work to serve the needs of her man. Lillian goes to work to support Jay; Hedja becomes Molnar's source of financial support as well as his muse. "He permits her love to flow all around him, sustain him, nourish him." Through maternal solicitude, Hedja becomes stronger than her husband, who has actually suppressed her femininity in his efforts to make her a lady in their "strange marriage of his feminine qualities with her masculine ones." Molnar's fear of Hedja's sensuality, her primitiveness, her appetites is expressed in sexual parsimony, "a severe economy of pleasure. She is often left hungry."[7]

Nevertheless, Hedja begins to grow. She develops into an aggressive woman. Terrified of losing her support, Molnar criticizes her, significantly denying her ladylikeness. " 'Your ambitions are vulgar.' " In conflict, Hedja hopes, "Perhaps Molnar will turn about now and protect her. It is the dream of every maternal love: I have filled him with my strength. I have nourished his painting. My painting has passed into his painting. I am broken and weak. Perhaps now he will be strong."[8]

But Molnar does not return what he has received. Instead, he replaces Hedja with another woman. Now that she has been abandoned—or liberated—Hedja continues to pursue her own unveiling. As the veils are lifted she becomes boastful, grandiose, competitive, and self-centered. Hedja becomes "inflated physically and spiritually." Nin concludes the story by showing how Hedja regresses to her original state as a "child of nature and succulence and sweets, of pillows and erotic literature. The frogs leap away in fear of her again."[9] Hedja's paintings grow larger, but not better. They reveal her willful return to primitive self-assertion.

"Hedja" represents a transitional period in Anaïs Nin's life. The fear that it expresses about woman's nature was gradually overcome as Nin worked out her concept of woman, prescribing the obligation each person has to transform his or her destructive impulses into positive actions. Nin's view of woman is quite explicit as she expresses it in "Notes on Feminism" of 1972. Men and women alike must become aware of their dangerous tendencies, then learn to translate this negative energy into beneficial actions or productive projects. This is easier for woman because the centuries-old image of the "lady" has demanded the repression of aggression and anger. Yet as woman frees herself from this restrictive model of behavior there is a danger that she may lose control of her negative emotions.

Something valuable appears in "Hedja" to balance the anxiety this story expresses about the nature of woman once unveiled; this is the discovery that woman, like man, *can* in fact be irresponsible, destructive, and even cruel. To recover this belief is to recover a lost power along with a more exciting and more complex image of woman than the suffering virgin idealized by Christianity.

The themes of "Hedja" represent a breakthrough in Nin's thought. The image of woman is much like that presented in Rank's essay, but the disturbing conclusion—that woman's assertion of her naked self may become an irresponsible display of selfishness and narcissism—is one that does not represent Nin's permanent point of view. While it is true that woman, once liberated, might be as inflated with self as is Hedja, this is not a necessary outcome. The positive discovery of "Hedja" is the recovery of an image of strength; it is the idea that woman possesses her own source of vitality and direct relation to creation without the need to rely indefinitely on man. This rediscovery of woman's power allows her to imagine herself as capable of certain achievements without fearing herself to be masculine.

A study of what Anaïs Nin feared to lose in the process of becoming an artist is extremely valuable for the light shed on general problems of creative women. The question of sexual identity is central to many of these problems. Woman is expected to devote her life to procreation, not creation. If she refuses to do this, shame and guilt are bound to haunt her; they are entwined with the threat of losing femininity. In *The Way of All Women,* M. Esther Harding states that "From the very beginning of our civilization there has been a widespread conviction that women cannot create, a conviction that it is in some obscure way almost indecent for them to do so. The conventional attitude suggests that creativeness is the prerogative of the man while for a woman to put forth something she herself has conceived and created is to disregard her instinctive reticence and modesty."[10] Lawrence J. Hatterer, one of the few male psychologists to write about the woman artist, concentrates upon the threat to her sexual identity:

> She has to decide how far to carry her talent without losing the feminine identity she has assigned to herself. If she competes more aggressively, if she dares too much or creates with abandon, she runs the risk of isolation from both sexes. When she is insistent, she is considered aggressive, masculine, odd. If she is single, she is classified as a woman who could not succeed as wife and mother and is fearful of these roles. If she is married, she is made to feel guilty about the need for an artistic identity; she is told that to maintain this identity will ruin her children or destroy her marriage. It is only with grim de-

termination, competitive, even castrating maneuvering, a sort of underground living, that she emerges free to follow her course.[11]

In his book *Art and Artist* Rank brings out an aspect of the creator's psychic makeup that does much to clarify the reasons the woman artist suffers so intensely from the conflict between procreation and creation. Rank describes the nature of the creative or productive personality and carefully distinguishes it from that of the neurotic type. He then identifies and analyzes the artist's fear and frequent avoidance of procreation. "This problem . . . only becomes intelligible through the conception of immortality—as it is represented biologically in sexual propagation—by the individual immortality of deliberate self-perpetuation [in a work of art]."[12] Rank's "productive" personality type has created himself through an act of will; he substitutes an artificial type of creation, art, for instinctive bodily procreation. This type engages in activity that furnishes the illusion of living longer than his physical body can possibly do. Procreation, on the other hand, is an implicit acknowledgment of death. This is bitter, even unacceptable, for the artist, who has mobilized his will to transform himself into an instrument of productivity precisely in order to transcend his mortality, thereby achieving the illusion of projecting his existence beyond the duration of the body. Apart from practical considerations of time, energy, and money, the bearing and raising of children is a constant reminder of mortality; it is a denial of everything the artist has wagered his existence against. If the male artist usually wishes to avoid procreation, so, too, will the female artist. (In "Silences," Tillie Olsen has pointed out how few women artists of significant achievement were married or had children.[13]) But how much the greater will be *her* anguish at giving up motherhood, since it is what she has been trained for since birth. She will have to choose, and whichever choice she makes will result in special problems.

From using one's "goodness" in mothering children to using it to attract and hold men is but a small step, we have seen in the

preceding chapter. Lawrence J. Hatterer has stated that the successful woman artist antagonizes men. Most males are accustomed to
deriving a sense of masculine confidence from successful competition—with other men and with women. If a woman is superior,
particularly in work that brings her fame or money, men are almost certain to identify her as "masculine" and exclude her from
their range of emotional interest. Explaining her fear of publishing
her Diary, Anaïs Nin wrote: "I associated honesty with the loss of
love. The only women I had known who were honest, belligerent,
assertive, undisguised had lost love. I was not going to risk that."[14]
When she entered analysis with René Allendy Nin said she wanted
to become a writer because she thought she would be more interesting to men. Perhaps unconsciously she wished to flatter and disarm the analyst with this confession, or perhaps, in her innocence
and youthful romanticism, she truly did believe a woman artist
would be fascinating to men. In either case, this statement exposes
Nin's anxiety about fusing the identities of woman and creator.
This anxiety did not disappear, even as she made progress toward
her goal. Even after she had successfully overcome many inner
obstacles, she proclaimed: "The drama of woman's development is
very painful, for in each case the man seems to punish all growth."[15]

Deeply related to her fear of alienating men and therefore losing
their admiration and love, Anaïs Nin feared the sort of masculiniza-
tion of herself that she associated with actions that seemed to her
destructive. This conflict is also experienced by Anna Wulf in Doris
Lessing's novel *The Golden Notebook*. The goodness that woman
has repeatedly been told is her finest quality and the one most indispensable to her womanliness is often an obstacle to the free expression of her energies in creative work. Nin was deeply resistant
to taking on any "masculine" qualities; for a time this resistance
actually prevented her from writing novels; her diary was "feminine"; novels "masculine." Henry Miller and, later, Gonzalo More
both tried to help Nin understand that she would have to be less
"good" to others if she were to do what she wanted to do in life.
Gonzalo challenged:

"You never let yourself explode. You put all kinds of obstacles in your own way, they are all obstacles, lids, restrictions, all your loves are devotions, services, keeping you from exploding. You have drowned your strength. You hamper and block yourself."

"It is not compatible with being a woman. Within all these boundaries, restrictions, I do what I want," [she replied.]

"Yes, you do, magnificently. You do all you want except to live for yourself. Your care not to destroy anything takes all your energy and ingenuity and imagination."[16]

Gonzalo was right.

Otto Rank, however, presented his patient with an opposed point of view: "Rank believes that to create it is necessary to destroy. Woman cannot destroy. He believes that may be why she has rarely been a great artist. In order to create without destroying, I nearly destroyed myself." At this period of her life Nin evidently depended on Rank to motivate her to complete her writing: "Rank made me finish *House of Incest*. He helped me to discover the meaning and then I was able to make a synthesis."[17] If the artist truly must be capable of destruction to create, how then could any "womanly" woman hope to become a creator? Rank presented Nin with the alternatives of becoming a woman (strengthening her feminine self-confidence) or an artist:

'Women,' said Rank, 'when cured of neurosis, enter life. Man enters art. Woman is too close to life, too human.' The feminine quality is necessary to the male artist, but Rank questioned whether masculinity is equally necessary to the woman artist.

At this point, when I became a woman, I glowed with womanliness: I was expansive, relaxed, happy.

Rank said, looking at me admiringly, 'You look entirely different today.' I felt as soft as a summer day, all bloom and scent, all joy of being.

'Perhaps,' he said, 'you may discover now what you want—
to be a woman or an artist.'[18]

This presentation of alternatives may well have been a part of
Rank's strategy as analyst. In any case, Nin was wise enough to
reject the necessity of choice, with its essential reductiveness. She
continued working toward the expansion of her identity that she
desired, and finally attained.

A fascinating and disturbing aspect of Anaïs Nin's conflict over
"masculinity" involves the attribution of feminine gender to her
diary. "Rank thinks my diary invaluable as a study of woman's
point of view. He says it is a document by a woman who thinks as
a woman, not like a man." This entry was made in 1935. For some
time Nin divided writing into feminine and masculine types. She
felt comfortable with the former, deeply ill-at-ease with, even hostile to, the latter: "I must continue the diary because it is a feminine
activity, it is a personal and personified creation, the opposite of
the masculine alchemy. I want to remain on the untransmuted, un-
transformed, untransposed plane. This alchemy called creation, or
fiction, has become for me as dangerous as the machine." Because
in the diary experience was protected against loss, this writing was
feminine, i.e., maternal. The hard, polished quality, the finality of
a conventional piece of fiction disturbed Nin, who had endowed
motion with great significance, making it a necessary requisite of
living forms. So, though she continued to *want* to write fiction, the
obstacle remained: "Conflict with diary-writing. While I write in
the diary I cannot write a book. I try to flow in a dual manner, to
keep recording and to invent at the same time, to transform. The
two activities are antithetical."[19] While her continued devotion to
the diary emphasized Anaïs Nin's femininity, she was still frustrated
in her desire to write the kinds of books she could present to the
public. One reason for this was her unconquered fear of becoming,
or seeming to be, masculine.

It was not until 1944, nine years after Rank had suggested that
the diary was feminine, that Anaïs Nin was able to sustain the diary
and fiction simultaneously. This became possible only after a break-

down in New York in 1942 and Nin's subsequent treatment by a
third analyst, Martha Jaeger. This therapist gradually assisted her
patient in consolidating an artistic identity that included powers
regarded by the world as masculine.

Dr. Jaeger was recommended by Moira, a friend whose character seems to have suggested that of Hedja. Jaeger was a Jungian,
and under her direction Anaïs Nin was able further to weaken the
hold on her unconscious of the Christian ideal of the saintly, self-
sacrificing woman. Gradually she adopted the model of the more
complex, multifaceted woman whose roots are in nature and who
acknowledges her capacity for destruction (the "primitive" who is
studied in "Hedja"). The most valuable concept of Jungian psychology for the aspiring woman artist is the figure of the animus, the
"personification of the masculine nature of a woman's [uncon-
scious]. This psychological bisexuality is a reflection of the biological fact that it is the larger number of male (or female) genes which
is the decisive factor in the determination of sex. The smaller number of contrasexual genes seems to produce a corresponding contrasexual character, which usually remains unconscious."[20] Jung's
idea of psychological bisexuality provides both the theory and the
dynamics of a process through which an individual can strengthen
herself by bringing unconscious "masculine" powers into consciousness and integrating them with other aspects of the self. In this respect, Jung's theory of personality provides an ideal of self-suffi-
ciency and psychic wholeness, as well as a process for achieving
both.

Rank did not believe that masculinity is "necessary to the
woman artist." Whatever he meant by "masculinity," Rank underestimated his patient's need to develop qualities of strength in commitment to writing. After her maternal activities grew beyond her
control, robbing her of money, energy, and time, and Nin broke
down, she wrote in her diary: "It seemed to me that I was broken
for good, physically and spiritually." In April of 1944, a few months
after starting work with Jaeger, a very different sounding Nin records her ideal of a new image of woman.[21] She is Valentina Orli-
kova, the first female captain of the Soviet merchant navy. "A pho-

tograph of her had appeared, which all of us fell in love with. Short dark hair, regular features but fleshly and sensuous, beautiful dark eyes, clear-cut and stylized in her captain's uniform. She conveyed firmness and capability, without hardness or coldness. She became a symbol of woman's most secret wishes: to be able to be free and in command of her own destiny, responsible, without loss of her womanliness."[22]

This ideal of the womanly but free and self-sufficient female has remained unchanged in Nin's thought. The problem that required solution if she herself were to become this sort of woman was one of balance. The feminine identity Nin had formed and strengthened under Rank's guidance was based upon her generosity to others; this had to be greatly reduced if she were to translate her own energy into art. But the idea that she might do less for others threatened Nin with the loss of their love. "Creation and femininity seemed incompatible. The *aggressive* act of creation. 'Not aggressive,' said Jaeger. '*Active*.' I have a horror of the masculine 'career' woman. To create seemed to me such an assertion of the strongest part of me that I would no longer be able to give all those I love the feeling of their being stronger, and they would love me less."[23] Gradually, by turning away little by little from some of her more demanding "children," Nin claimed a greater part of her life for herself and conceived the project of *Cities of the Interior*. This was a triumph, since previously, novel-writing had threatened Nin with its seeming "masculinity." Now she could accept her own involvement with, even commitment to, work she regarded as masculine.

The process which enabled Anaïs Nin to consolidate her identity as a writer involved a series of intense relationships with creative men, usually writers. In *Art and Artist* Rank makes a persuasive presentation of how people who feel themselves to be incomplete form relationships based on identification with another person who possesses the necessary or desired qualities. In this light, Rank analyzes the artist's dependence on his muse and certain homosexual relationships which are "less a sexual perversion than an ego-problem . . . a problem with which the individual can only deal by personifying a portion of his own ego in another individual."[24] The process Rank describes seems similar to phases in the movement toward self-realization which, in a Jungian context, would be either the actualization of the shadow or the implementation of the anima or animus. One can see in both *House of Incest* and *Ladders to Fire* Nin's own dramatization of this psychic action; the "I" of the prose poem and the two women in *Ladders* seek self-completion through fusion. This would be the recognition of the shadow, for the two in these psychic dramas are of the same sex.

While growing into her self-chosen identity as artist, Anaïs Nin had much assistance, support, and encouragement from male writers. While she was in Paris during the 1930's they were the father figures, analysts, writers or both, whose guidance she sought. Nin's father was, of course, an artist, but identification with him was difficult because of his selfishness; as Nin perceived him, he was the man who had abandoned her when she was a child. Besides René Allendy, Nin's first important friendships with creative men were with Miller and Rank, both of whom were so different from her father in so many ways that she could experience the pleasure of rebellion at the same time that she enjoyed friendships with creative men who had an interest in her well-being and a wish to encourage her writing ambitions. As she grew stronger in her feminine role, more the mother than the daughter, Nin became less dependent on Miller's and Rank's direction. In fact, she became critical of Miller and, in a more tender spirit, amused by some of Rank's personal foibles. With independence came a capacity to criticize these former personifications of wisdom, if not authority.

In New York during the 1940s and 50s, Anaïs Nin formed close relationships with several male writers. Poets usually, they were young; among the best-known are Robert Duncan and James Leo Herlihy. Her friendships with such men as these gave Nin psychic complements, animus figures whose qualities of sensitivity and love of writing helped her maintain her own writing endeavors. She could coordinate her creative work with that of a man with whom she could identify in many ways and who would not threaten her autonomy, as Miller tried to do and, later, Edmund Wilson would have done by trying to mold her talent to his personal literary values. The muse, Rank argues, must be someone who is sexually distant. "For the other woman, whom, from purely human or other motives, he perhaps loves more, he often enough cannot set up as his Muse for this very reason: that she would thereby become in a sense de-feminized and, as it were, made into an object (in the egocentric sense) of friendship. To the Muse for whom he creates (or thinks he creates), the artist seldom gives himself; he pays with his work . . ."[25]

If one substitutes the feminine for the masculine pronouns in this passage, it becomes clear, I think, why friendships with homosexual writers and artists have been so important to Nin. (The supreme muse, for Nin, is Marcel Proust.) Incarnations of her animus, these men served as muses to the developing woman artist as she, no doubt, helped bring into consciousness the anima figure. She seems, if indirectly, to have realized this when, in *Diary V*, she wrote: "Relationship to the airy young men (unreal, remote, nonhuman) is over because it was my relationship to a volatile, airy, nonhuman father. I now accept my friendships with serious, earthbound men, my comfortable relationships with women . . ."[26]

It is questionable to what extent Jung himself acknowledged the woman's power to be a creator. He seemed to interpret the animus qualities as giving the woman the power to assist a man in achieving his projects—in short, to play the muse: "Just as a man brings forth his work as a complete creation out of his inner feminine nature, so the inner masculine side of a woman brings forth creative seeds which have the power to fertilize the feminine side of the man. This would be the *femme inspiratrice* . ."[27] It was Emma Jung, herself a psychoanalyst, who understood that the role of muse might not be enough to satisfy a creative woman. She described the influence of the animus as applying directly to the psychic development of the woman. "What is really necessary is that the feminine intellectuality, logos in the woman, should be so fitted into the nature and life of the woman that a harmonious cooperation between the feminine and masculine factors ensues and no part is condemned to a shadowy existence."[28]

In achieving this harmonious cooperation between the feminine and masculine dimensions, Nin seems to have gained much support from Robert Duncan's friendship. They appear to have related to each other in various ways: as friends, mother and son, twins or soulmates. Emma Jung explains that the animus is likely to appear as a boy, a son or a young friend when the woman's "own masculine component is thus indicated as being in a state of becoming."[29] Nin and Duncan encouraged each other's writing. Reading her Diary inspired him. They actually wrote together, in the same room. "Robert is back. So the two typewriters are clicking in unison again." At the height of their closeness, Nin and Duncan exchanged diaries. More surprising still, they actually made entries in each other's diaries; this suggests the depth of their identification with each other. When Duncan became too selfish a "child" though, placing upon her the same demands that others did, Nin was forced to preserve herself by pushing him away—but with what a sense of grief. "I lost Robert because I could not feed him. It was the second time I refused to take on a burden. And so I lost him."[30]

Soon after the break with Duncan, Martha Jaeger told Nin: " 'All you are trying to do is throw off this mother role imposed on you. You want a give-and-take relationship.' "[31] Although Nin continued to seek psychological support for her art through friendships with male writers, her subsequent friends did not disappoint her as deeply as Duncan. The freest and most equally balanced of these relationships seems to have been one with James Leo Herlihy; it is described in the fifth and sixth Diaries. Particularly vivid and interesting are the letters exchanged by Nin and Herlihy between 1955 and 1966.

Except for artist Frances Field, Nin does not seem to have been close to women creators until she had reconciled her conflict between "masculinity" and productivity and had begun to feel comfortable with her sense of maturity as a woman and writer. In *Diary V* powerful and self-possessed women artists begin to appear. They are described with liking and admiration: Sylvia Beach; composer Bebe Barron; Lesley Blanch, author of *The Wilder Shores of Love* (biographies of four women who led adventurous lives); Jane Bowles; Shirley Clark; Caresse Crosby; Maya Deren; Martha

Graham and Djuna Barnes (both heroines for Nin); Anna Kavan; Josephine Premice; Mary Caroline Richards; Marguerite Young. Of special importance during the years 1947-1955 were friendships with the sculptor Cornelia Runyon; with composer Peggy Glanville-Hicks, whom Nin greatly admires; and Renate Druks, the model for the most prominent figure in *Collages*. This new closeness to creative women continues through the years of *Diary VI,* which includes affectionate portraits of poet Daisy Aldan; Drs. Anita Faatz and Virginia P. Robinson, founders of the Otto Rank Society; author and translator, Louise Varèse; meetings with Maude Hutchins and Marguerite Duras, and, of course, the continuation of sustaining friendships with Frances Field and Marguerite Young. It seems clear that Nin became free to round out her identity as a specifically "feminine" creator only after she had succeeded in implementing the "masculine" qualities she once so greatly feared.

Nin's development as an artist shows both sides of the process of moving toward self-realization by bringing both masculine and feminine components of the self into the sort of awareness that can result in changed actions. The recognition of her animus demanded that she put increasing emphasis on her commitment to writing at the risk of sacrificing personal relationships. At the same time, Nin was becoming more aware of her own femininity, or what it was she as a woman could achieve in writing that would be difficult for a male writer. Like many intuitive people, she was conscious of her direction for some time before she had developed the capacity to pursue it. Challenged by Miller's and Durrell's constant urgings that she write more "realistically," Nin began instead to search for specifically feminine values in writing. In August of 1939 after a long discussion with Miller and the Durrells, Nin recorded in her diary a lengthy statement that articulates her ideals as a consciously "feminine" writer. The goal, as she sees it, is a fusion of life and artistic creation in the energy of the womb, a metaphor for the woman's approach to art that was stimulated by Nin's first visit to Fez in Morocco. Woman's creation must be "human," not abstract (separated from nature), for its purpose is to reconnect the vital links between human life and the natural world, or to re-create the unity that man has "destroyed by his proud consciousness." Nin criticizes Miller because "Henry's creation at times resembles insanity, because it is experience disconnected from feeling—like an anesthetized soul injected with ether." The restoration of this lost unity requires a journeying back toward the primitive, toward the "bad earth too, the demon, the instincts, the storms of nature. Tragedies, conflicts, mysteries are personal."[32] Woman's writing must be personal because it must balance the detached, impersonal works of man.

The mission of recovering human authenticity and the dynamic connections to powerful instincts is dangerous. If man has been destructive because of his contempt for nature, and for woman, whom he identifies with nature, woman can be destructive because of her closeness to these powers. Man's drive to tame and civilize instinct kills his vitality, splits him into parts, drives feelings underground, and ends by producing an incomplete and therefore false view of reality. Woman's drive to be free again, free from the veils, the cumbersome clothing and the exaggerated refinement that man has imposed upon her can lead to irresponsible acts of cruelty simply because they are "natural." But energy always lends itself to transformation; it can be used as its possessor wishes. Again and again Nin has stressed her belief that the transformation of negative impulses into positive ones is the responsibility of all individuals, but especially of the artist whose life project is the preservation, interpretation, and transformation of his personal experiences.

Woman's task, then, as Nin sees it, is to restore balance to the human composition by repudiating the false images of femininity invented for her by man, by asserting her own authentic nature as she herself experiences it, and by expressing this authentic woman in her life projects, including, of course, her art. Woman's creation is a work of restoration, and the first job is the rediscovery and proclamation of woman's nature as it arises from her knowledge of herself. Nin wrote that man "disposed of her [woman] by identifying her with nature and then paraded his contemptuous domination of nature. But woman is not nature only. She is the mermaid with her fish-tail dipped in the unconscious. Her creation will be to make articulate this obscure world which dominates man, which he denies being dominated by, but which asserts its domination in destructive proofs of its presence, madness."[33]

Because its expressive content is different, feminine literary style will necessarily be different from that of programmatically masculine writers. Feminine writing, does not, of course, have to be practiced by women. The point is not who does it but the nature and approach to the subject. Feminine art restores connections with nature; instead of dominating her materials, the artist coaxes them to reveal their essences. In describing the sculpture of Cornelia Runyon, Nin has written, "From the first she had an essentially feminine attitude towards her material. She began with a respect for what the sea or the earth had already begun to form in the stones. She contemplated and meditated over them, permitting them to reveal the the inherent patterns they suggested. She never imposed her own will over the image tentatively begun by nature."[34] Feminine art stresses feelings instead of thought processes: "I choose the heightened moments, because they bring to bear all the forces of intuition. For this I choose moods, states of being, states of exaltation, to accentuate the reality of feeling and the senses. It is this that I contribute to a feminine concept: the language of emotion, altogether different from that of intellect."[35]

Since feminine art seeks to link up, to relate, to reveal the connections between the diverse aspects of life, it must flow, resisting all tendencies to harden and crystallize. (The belief that writing that is alive *flows* prevented Anaïs Nin from writing conventional novels, but eventually it led her to invent more organic forms of prose.) To achieve the desired sense of quickness, the immediacy of writing that arises directly from feelings, Nin stresses spontaneity and improvisation. The writer who wishes to stress feelings and to present character and theme with a sense of animation will, in all likelihood, experiment with language in order to project states of consciousness into the depths that are concealed by the words and gestures, the surfaces of visual reality.

It is true, of course, that these literary ideals are by no means exclusively feminine; the roots of Nin's art lie in the Symbolist movement and, to a lesser extent, in the Surrealist program for revolution of consciousness. It is just as true that not all women writers will be temperamentally sympathetic to the ideals Nin has identified as "feminine." The significance of her statements about woman's art, besides their being a description after the fact, a critical explanation of what she was already doing, is that this outpouring of ideals represented the bringing into consciousness of values that needed to be articulated. Whether "feminine" or not—and perhaps gender is irrelevant to styles in art—Nin's literary values have for too long been neglected, especially in the United States. The fact that she has expressed these values in so many ways places her at the center of a new movement, perhaps a countermovement, in American literature. Traditionally, writing that is intuitive, introspective, delicate, tentative, explorative, meditative, has been ridiculed as "precious" or "feminine"; this fact says more about our cultural values than about literature itself. Nin's statement of her beliefs, her articulate opposition to Miller and Durrell, gave her courage, once she saw her own thoughts in words. And now this courage has spread to other writers, male and female alike, who feel a greater confidence in their "sensitive" orientation toward writing. *The Novel of the Future* is "dedicated to sensitive Americans. May they create a sensitive America."

One of the kinds of courage Nin has gained through the years is a sense of justification in writing about herself as a woman. In this Rank encouraged her, as did Durrell. Surprising as it seems, few women writers, even great ones, have challenged the conventional, male-defined concepts of woman. They, too, have perpetuated the stereotypes, that tedious line of saints and sinners enshrined in most fiction of the past. Discovering the nature of woman is, as Rank confessed, a vast project for the future. Psychologists and writers may be expected to bring special talents to this task. As for Nin, once her sense of self as artist began to grow, she was able to formulate her purpose in writing *Cities of the Interior:*

> Theme of development of woman in her own terms, not as an imitation of man. This will become in the end the predominant theme of the novel: the effort of woman to find her own

psychology, and her own significance, in contradiction to man-made psychology and interpretation. Woman finding her own language, and articulating her own feelings, discovering her own perceptions. Woman's role in the reconstruction of the world. . . . The evolution will be from subjectivity and neurosis to objectivity, expansion, fulfillment.[36]

One of the best ways to measure the growth of Anaïs Nin as she conceptualized the idea of woman as artist is to compare two of her important characters, Stella in the novelette that bears her name and Renate in *Collages*. Written in 1944 when the author was thinking about a series of interconnected novels and struggling with the psychological dimensions of woman's problems as artist, "Stella" explores the failure of connection between the artist's personal life and her work; this failure is caused by a neurosis that is unchallenged, a childishness that is not outgrown. As a movie star Stella is much more glamorous, vital, self-assured, and daring than in private life. The contrast is so great that when she sits in the audience watching one of her own films, she is never recognized. Stella's closets are filled with dramatic hats and shoes she dares not wear. The most important object in her apartment is a "very large, very spacious Movie Star bed of white satin," which she usually occupies alone.[37]

Stella is unhappy in her relationships with men. She demands too much of Bruno, who is married. Even though Stella recognizes that she herself could not be a wife, she gradually increases her demands on Bruno's time and affections until he withdraws from her. Stella's preoccupation with her own needs and her inability to comprehend Bruno except in relation to herself destroy their once-delightful love. Stella's second relationship with Philip contains even less emotional nourishment. Still wholly absorbed in self-pity, Stella misinterprets not only her self but also those of the people she meets. Having chosen Philip because she thinks he is different from the other men she has known, Stella discovers that he is the exact image of her father, a selfish Don Juan whose behavior is destructive to women.

Because Stella is too preoccupied with her misery to commit herself to growth and challenge in her art, her work does not sustain her. Falsely feminine in her preference for the personal over the professional, Stella lacks responsibility toward her work. "No matter how exigent was the demand made upon Stella by her screen work, she always overthrew every obstacle in favor of love." But love fails her. The most moving moment in the novelette is the portrait of Stella waiting for Bruno to telephone. Typically neurotic, she longs for him, even though she has driven him away. She had made up her mind not to answer his call. Her gratification will come from the fact that the man felt a desire to talk to her or be with her.

Eventually, the poverty of her inner life harms her career. Stella's public image hardens as she retreats deeper and deeper into herself, losing her former animation: "She appeared in a new story on the screen. Her face was immobile like a mask. It was not Stella. It was the outer shell of Stella."[38] The flow that Anaïs Nin has always sought between the personal life and the artistic life does not occur for Stella. Like others, she has been hurt by her childhood, but she has done nothing to repair this damage, nothing to inspire her own growth. Her narcissistic distortion of her personal reality swells beyond control. Stella is left tiny and lost in the midst of this empty inflation.

Renate, the painter at the center of *Collages* (published in 1964, twenty years after "Stella" was written) is as genuinely alive as Stella at first appears to be. Wherever she goes, Renate brings people, even objects, to life, endowing the still with gestures, the silent with voices, bringing out the features of the masked and veiled. *Collages* opens with Renate's animating the statues of Vienna by imagining them in motion. Always warmly responsive, Renate accepts other people's faults and limitations. She is never judgmental. She is fluid, and fluent too, qualities that Anaïs Nin particularly admires.

The man in *Collages* is Bruce; he is charming but indolent and bisexual. Travel by houseboat through Holland and France finds Renate busy bailing while Bruce reads or sleeps. When a fire threatens to destroy their home, Bruce rescues a large portrait of himself. His cruelty comes out when he writes short narratives of

his homosexual past including some that reveal his sadistic tendencies; Bruce hides these in Chinese boxes, inviting Renate to read
them when she wishes to know him better. What she reads makes
Renate angry. She hurls some of the boxes into the sea and burns
others. After a time though, she recovers from her disappointment.
She does not reject Bruce, but accepts what he can give. Renate's
life is filled with much besides this relationship. Painting, many
friendships, travel, all make her life very active and all her activities are interconnected, nourishing one another. Renate is far
healthier and more mature than Stella. At the same time, she is
free from the guilt that weighs down Djuna and Lillian.

Renate is the most fully developed example of Anaïs Nin's concept of femininity and art. The combination of a creative attitude
toward people (helping to evoke atmospheres in which others are
free to be themselves) and her devotion to the art of painting make
her the single figure in Nin's fiction whose life expresses the values
described in the Diaries as specifically feminine. Collectively, these
are associated with the principle of Eros: seeking relationships and
connections, placing human concerns before abstract ones, maintaining a constant awareness of other people through the use of
empathy and intuition. Renate's touch is light, and it bestows life.
Like her creator, Renate has "to turn destruction into creation over
and over again."[39] Renate is complex, but her being is unified by a
strong center. Of her real-life prototype, Nin wrote: "Renate can
penetrate any experience or role without dissolution of her self.
They are extensions, dilations, expansions, not dissolutions. She
can play various roles with none disconnected from each other. She
is as fluid as mercury, which can move in all directions and yet not
be divided."[40]

The ending of *Collages* may well be prophetic. Renate and a Dr.
Mann insistently rescue a woman writer from self-imposed solitude
caused by public misunderstanding and neglect of her work. She is
Judith Sands, the author of several books, at least one of which is
great. She has barricaded herself inside her apartment, refusing to
unlock her door to admirers. Together, Dr. Mann and Renate coax

her forth to accompany them to the Museum of Modern Art for a "happening" in the Sculpture Garden.

At the museum the three become part of a crowd that watches a bizarre event. A huge heap of trash that has been wired by its collector, Tinguely, begins to burn, a part at a time. As it burns it emits rolls of paper on which a huge brush paints the names of artists and writers. Sometimes the rolls are sucked back into the apparatus. When the last part catches fire and explodes, the crowd scrambles for the bits and pieces of paper. The names of many artists are destroyed, but Dr. Mann salvages a slip which retains the name of Judith Sands. This suggests that her books will outlive the era of destructive technology, an era in which a man like Tinguely actually nudges his own brainchild to death by giving it a final kick.

It is different with Judith Sands. Won over by her new friends, she invites them to her apartment for a drink. There she consents to show them a manuscript. It begins with the same words as does *Collages*. There is an unbroken line from one woman writer to another, a connection whose existence suggests the possibility of a future history of women writers. This is the tradition whose absence seemed so damaging to Virginia Woolf forty-some years ago when she wrote *A Room of One's Own*.

Not only Renate but also Dr. Mann rescue Judith Sands and reassure her of her value as an artist. Dr. Mann has come all the way from Israel near Persia (Iran) where Hedja was first veiled; he comes to seek a meeting with Judith Sands. In her powerful art she has actually created him in the personage of one of her characters. He is "man enough" to recognize and applaud her. Hopefully, women and men alike will participate in recognizing the woman creator. And eventually the time will come when women writers will no longer keep their manuscripts in black boxes, partly to hide them and partly to protect them from the eyes of the world.

Once Anaïs Nin hid her magnificent diary in just this way.[41]

Anaïs: Her Book

> My dear Diary, it is Anaïs who is speaking to you, and not someone who thinks as everybody should think. Dear Diary, pity me, but listen to me.
> —*The Diary of Anaïs Nin, Volume I*

There are perhaps as many motives as there are diarists, persons pledged to confide to the covers of a journal intended only for its author's eyes the data of life: accounts received; rages suppressed; passions inflamed or dying; dreams of being noticed, or freed, or invited to share another's private prison. The project of writing a book for an audience of one, one's self at that, intrigues, with its many-faceted possibilities, a great variety of authors both professional and unprofessional. Some use a diary strictly as a record: to document the facts of their existence or to preserve particularly interesting experiences lest they slide away with memory. Such diarists are the savers, the hoarders, those thrifty persons whose records can always be relied upon for names and dates, for accurate details. Other diarists are deep, inhibited persons, whom life denies sufficient occasions for self-expression and who are, consequently, thrown back upon their privacy in order to touch the reality of their existence in the re-creation of words. Such are the imprisoned: criminals, especially political prisoners, or the restless children of limited or tyrannical parents. Others, experiencing an awakening of self, may turn to a diary for temporary companionship, as adolescent girls often do, to record the confusion and awe of passing

117

from one phase of life to another. A third group of diarists are the latter-day romantics, persons whose natures require extreme experiences, ecstatic moods, and intense responses. If they are unfortunate enough to be born in an age of pragmatist values and materialist achievements, these persons of romantic temperament may become diarists in order to express their secret selves, the selves that are out of fashion, inappropriate, or ridiculous in the eyes of the solid citizens who rule the world. Anyone with an inner life that cannot be expressed in actions may easily become a diligent diarist.

Anaïs Nin has kept her Diary for all these reasons. Dreading to lose precious experience through time, she has recorded in her diary everything she wished to preserve. She has suffered the discomfort of being a dreamer in a culture that despises the dreamer for his idleness and impracticality, and an artist in a society that distrusts his defense of beauty and fears the exposure of his perceptions. Nin has used her Diary as a place to express her fantasies, her ambitions, her terrors, and joys. Seldom allowing herself to convey anger and hostility personally, Nin has entrusted her violent moods to her Diary. "All of us have our demons. Mine is caged in the diary. That may be why I so often dream that the diary is burning."[1] The form of a diary is organic, its tone intimate. It offers room for as many styles of writing as exist, as many types of entries the diarist wishes to include. It is an ideal writer's notebook, a treasury of characters, incidents, and themes. Besides helping Anaïs Nin perfect her style, her diary has been the friend and companion of her desperate confidences. As a child of thirteen she personified it: "My dear Diary, it is Anaïs who is speaking to you, and not someone who thinks as everybody should think. Dear Diary, pity me, but listen to me."[2]

As the years passed and Nin developed as a writer, she began to make her Diary a work of art. It was never a typical writer's notebook or the "sketchbook" into which Otto Rank at one time hoped to transform it. Nin's Diary gradually became a work in its own right, one with all the polish and distinction of art. As a woman, with responsibilities and obligations to others that often seemed more important than her personal concerns, Nin has used her Diary to fill out her life; it is a complement; it is the expression of the dimensions of her self that her life has not always had room for. Nin's Diary is a more authentic, certainly a more complete, deeper, and fuller expression of her self than the actual life she has lived. Although her reasons for keeping the Diary have changed somewhat through the years, her faithfulness to it would seem remarkable were it not for the fact that this Diary has come to represent a self, a more developed, a vaster and more powerful self than that of the woman who wrote in it.

It is well known that Anaïs Nin began her Diary as a child of eleven, discovering an ingenious way of maintaining continuity and personal exchange with her father in another country. Naturally, a child whose parents separate, the one angrily removing her children across an ocean to live on another continent, would receive a psychic shock. Jung has written that the commitment to self-realization is often the reaction to a trauma or wound.[3] As a child Nin's way of protecting the vividness of her former life, her past, the part of herself that was connected to her father, the artist, was to begin the diary as a connection with this life, from which she had been uprooted without her consent. The circumstances of what must have seemed an emotionally and culturally impoverished life in New York City kept the need for the Diary alive, as did the comfortable but limited life Nin had in the 1930s in Louveciennes, France. The need for the Diary deepened as Nin felt more sharply the restrictions of her environment and the frustrations arising from her struggle to define herself as a creator. Henry Miller and Otto Rank alike tried to convince Nin to give up the Diary, transferring the time and energy it absorbed to writing composed for the public. "First, he [Rank] seized upon the diary as a shell, and as a defense. Then he asked me not to write in it any more, and this was as difficult as asking a drug addict to do without his drugs."[4] Five years later the Diary still strikes its author as an addiction: "One day when I returned to the houseboat, I had left on my desk a page from my diary written long ago, but which still seemed to apply today. 'This diary is my drug and my vice. This is the moment when I take up the mysterious pipe and indulge in reflections. Instead of writing a book I lie back and I dream and talk to myself. A drug.' "[5]

Rank's treatment of Anaïs Nin seems to have been based partly on a strategy for helping her feel more feminine. Accordingly, when he saw her difficulty redefining the Diary as a sketchbook, he began to praise its "femininity." During those years when Nin was trying to consolidate a sense of her identity as a writer, she very much needed to be able to think of writing as womanly: "I must continue the diary because it is a feminine activity . . . What comes out of the factory: painting, sculpture, pottery, rugs, architecture, novels, I now regard with fear. It is too far from the truth of the moment."[6] Identifying spontaneity, fluidity, openness of form, stylistic inventiveness as "feminine," Nin was unable for some years to write "masculine" fiction without a sense of discomfort. At this time her need for the Diary depended partly upon its being a perfect medium for spontaneity because of its secrecy.[7] Trapped by her immersion in and sense of naturalness with the "feminine" diary, Nin was blocked in her attempts to reach beyond her private world to seek the connections that she craved with the world.

One solution seemed to be to publish the Diary. Nin began to explore this idea in the 1930s. The critic Stuart Gilbert praised her by saying that she had "the makings of a Proust." But he judged flatly: "This is too natural and will never be published. You ought to write a novel."[8] In 1937 Faber and Faber rejected the Diary. Later, a 600-page condensation was compiled for Maxwell Perkins; nearly twenty years afterwards Nin burned this version. She was determined to publish the Diary "intact" or not at all. The conflict represented by the attribution of genders to diary and novel-writing continued until Nin's treatment by Martha Jaeger in the early 1940s. Finally, she overcame the resistance she felt toward writing novels and accepted the Diary as a natural and probably permanent part of her life. Joyously, *Diary III* concludes: "Close the door and window upon the world for a moment, turn to the diary for all its musical notations, and begin another novel."[9]

In Nin's, as in all lives, exuberant self-confidence and the assurance of wholeness have not been consistent comforts. In the 1950s when her novels were being published but were receiving none or mostly unsympathetic reviews, she lost confidence in her fiction as the work that would break her "ostracism from the world." She returned to her plan of publishing the Diary. Selections were made for a single-volume edition. This was shown to Duell, Sloan and Pearce (publishers of *The Four-Chambered Heart*) and, for the second time, to Maxwell Perkins. After *A Spy in the House of Love* had been rejected by 127 publishers, Nin brought it out at her own expense, arranging for distribution by the British Book Centre. But *Spy* was not very successful either in sales or critical reception, and Nin became so despondent that she decided not to write any more novels. Fortunately, this mood of discouragement did not last. She wrote both *Seduction of the Minotaur* and *Collages,* which are her most original and smoothly realized works of fiction. Again, in the 1960s Nin renewed her attempt to gain a sympathetic publisher for the *Diary*. Some of the letters of rejection she received are printed in *Diary VI*. The project of bringing out the *Diary* was too vast for the resources of Alan Swallow (who was then re-issuing Nin's novels), but an agreement was finally negotiated between Swallow and Harcourt Brace Jovanovich. In 1966 the first volume appeared. This was the beginning of Nin's long-delayed public recognition. Her Diary is unique. There is nothing else like it in our literature, and we have not yet had an opportunity to read the entire work.[10]

Anaïs Nin's Diary is neither a diary in the usual sense—a candid, uncensored record of the events of a life—nor is it a work of fiction like the frankly autobiographical "novels" of writers like Leiris, Celine, or Henry Miller. From the 1930s on Nin clearly regarded her Diary not as a notebook but as a self-justifying and self-sustaining work. This is the implication of her having tried as early as 1937 to publish it. Furthermore, the individual notebooks were given titles or themes, "Les Mots Flottants," for example, or "A la recherche des jeux perdus." A typed version was made concurrently with the handwritten pages; the language was refined; parts were edited. Furthermore, Nin has admitted to heightening the events of her Diary, as Stuart Gilbert noted when he told her it could not be published. "If I were a real diarist, like Pepys or Amiel, I would be satisfied to record, but I am not, I want to fill in, transform, project, expand, deepen, I want this ultimate flowering that comes of creation."[11] In *The Novel of the Future* she remarks: "It was the fiction writer who edited the diary."[12] As readers we can never know the verifiable "truth" of the contents of Nin's Diary; we can never know the difference between what happened and what was recorded. Adding to this complication is the fact that the published version of Nin's Diary has been edited and is therefore different from the original notebooks. Some names have been changed and some persons have been omitted at their own request, as has any material that might make the author legally vulnerable. In this edited form, then, the Diary is even closer to fiction than are the original notebooks. The result is a continuous account of a life, an account that cannot be assigned to a genre (as much modern writing cannot) but displays the qualities both of fiction—in its heightened intensity, overall magnification of its materials and in its superb language—and of autobiography insofar as its contents are not invented but have been transcribed from life. The result is a work that is fascinating both in its candor and in its mystery. Nin's Diary tells us more perhaps than we have ever known about any human being, possibly including ourselves. The Diary contains the woman Anaïs; her entire self can be encompassed only by regarding the Diary as a part of this self. Anaïs Nin is, in a crucial sense, herself plus the Diary in which she has recorded an amazing number and variety of unlived as well as lived selves. And yet the great paradox of the Diary is that, though it tells us much more than we have known about any living person, it tells us far less than we would like to know.

It is this exposure of self, astonishing as it is, that has won for Anaïs Nin's Diary both its detractors and its admirers. There are readers who, identifying the self with the ego, turn away because of what they regard as a continuous display of self-love. Other readers are fascinated and instructed not only by the author's exposure and constant analysis of her self but also by the correspondence between the feelings and insights she has expressed and those that remain alive but mute within themselves. The many roles that we are obliged to play in life alienate us from ourselves because they often do not represent our authentic selves. Furthermore, total honesty about feelings is rarely possible; it is too dangerous. Life provides neither time nor opportunities for total self-expression. But a diary provides both—to those who are willing to serve it with discipline and love.

Nin's Diary is as close to a complete, comprehensive, and deep expression of a human life as any one can think of or even imagine, short of a transcribed record of consciousness. Even this would be incomplete because it would exclude the life of the unconscious, along with the interpretations that are essential to making the symbolic language of the unconscious coherent, understandable, and, therefore, useful. The world that Nin gives us in the Diary is as total as she can make it, given the need to protect the identities of some friends and relatives. Nin's world spans continents and extends from coast to coast. Her range of acquaintances includes an astonishing variety of people from simple workers to the great and famous artists and writers she knows in Paris, New York, and California.

We cannot know anyone so well in life as we can know Anaïs Nin the diarist. People never reveal themselves completely to any one person. To grasp the whole view, even of those we love, we would be obliged to obtain repeated exposures of the person in question glimpsed in an endless variety of relationships with others in an endless variety of settings, time zones, and situations. This composite view of herself is what Nin gives us in the Diary. She is like a mobile, using language to turn to the surface facets of her self that in most of us are hidden because we lack both her awareness of herself and other people and her capacity to express this awareness. In the Diaries Nin actually revolves like the dancer described in *House of Incest,* showing her many faces to the world as she circles in slow motion.

Each volume of the Diary represents a phase in the unfolding life of the artist who is its author. Everything she records is filtered through a sensibility as fragile as a spiderweb that vibrates to every nuance of feeling yet is as tensile as a construction of fine steel. The individual Diaries are self-sustaining, each with a movement and a structure of its own; yet each moves from one to another in a fluent prose that is filled with the details of cultural history as the personal story evolves in a depth that probes the unconscious along with the external world. Comparable in this respect to the individual novels of *Cities of the Interior,* the individual Diaries are autonomous works that nevertheless assume an enhanced value and a richer texture when each is seen in context of the overall composition.

Viewed as a design, the Diary may be said to represent a spiral circling in a clockwise direction that signifies creative motion. The spiral rises from the central point of Nin's self, the voice that controls the Diaries; this spiral signifies the relationship between unity and multiplicity; it is related to the mandala. The spiral is also associated with dances of incantation that are used for healing purposes, and thus remind us of the circling dancer who is evoked at the close of *House of Incest.* It reminds us as well of the elaboration of the spiral as a metaphor for the dream that is part of the final rhapsody of "The Voice." A symbol of the evolution of the universe and of personal growth, the spiral of Nin's Diaries sweeps into motion from the point of the self, the "I" whose power of perception makes possible the apprehension and the interpretation of all that we experience.

To many readers the first published Diary will always seem to be the best, the one that holds the reader the most powerfully. This is easy to explain. In being the first, Diary I has the advantage of announcing the unique qualities of the entire project. The impact of this book purely as confession can scarcely by underestimated. Hypnotically, it draws even a reluctant reader into the author's terrifying yet fascinating confusion, into the tangle of fears and desires, the sense of a psyche in labor (to use a perhaps impossible metaphor). The absorption with self seems unprecedented. For the introspective reader, it is a surprise that lures him deeper and deeper into the depths of Nin's personal reality, a maze of perceptions among which she gropes in an attempt to emerge with a lucid understanding of herself. But at first the revelation of feelings, the careful elucidation of Nin's own outpost on reality, is a shock. There is something almost distasteful about the way the diarist seems locked inside the prison of awareness. This poetically rendered expression of subjectivity becomes artful under the pressure of Anaïs Nin's constant insight and analysis. Yet the more she is able to analyze, the more lost she seems to become.

Even if Nin's personal expedition does not strike correspondences in the reader's experience, then the concept of search itself may well do so. Beneath its apparently unorganized flowing surface there lies concealed a traditional structure based upon the ancient theme of the search for a father. In this case the search is conducted not by a young man, as in the epics of the past, but by a woman whose quest is for the artist father she has lost, along with a way of life she yearns to recover. She forms relationships with a series of men who are father figures: Miller, René Allendy, Otto Rank. Miller's robust nature, his naturalness, his directness; above all, his commitment to writing were exactly opposed to Joaquin Nin's indirectness, artificiality, and exaggerated concern with etiquette and social proprieties. In allying herself with Miller in a partial defense of his values, Nin gained a great deal: a stimulating intellectual relationship; the satisfaction of rebelling against her father; and, most important, a friend who encouraged her to write, who took her work seriously, reading it and criticizing it, helping her to become a writer. Although René Allendy, Nin's first analyst, engaged her interest for a time, his approach to the therapy was too conventional to hold her for long. Nin moved on to establish a mutually helpful relationship with Otto Rank whose intellectuality captivated her and whose emotional vulnerability aroused her compassion. Rank received an opportunity to work with a brilliant, complex patient whose personal difficulties very closely matched the problems he wanted to study and write about. From Rank, Nin received not only the intellectually exciting companionship of a highly original mind, but also, as her treatment progressed, the strengthened sense of her feminine identity which she needed at this period of her life.

The struggle of *Diary I* is for birth. The book is permeated with a terrible sense of travail, a continuous expression of suffering that is sometimes nearly unbearable. This culminates in the author's description of agony as she is compelled to deliver a six-month-old stillborn child. The birth is achieved, mercifully. It is not that of the

infant but of the mother herself, marking her passage to womanhood. Rank indirectly acknowledged that his patient had been
healed, for he wrote to Nin: " 'I am dying now. Come to my rescue.' " And she did, even though this meant leaving behind in
France both her father, who was suffering from eczema, and Henry,
who was "struggling to launch his book [*Tropic of Cancer*]."[13] Reunited with her father both actually and symbolically, the griev-
ing daughter has transcended her desire for dependence and assumed her responsibilities as a woman.

The second Diary describes a period of sadness, disappointment,
and threatened loss. A different sort of struggle permeates its pages.
The structure arises from conflict, various types of conflict in an
interwoven presentation: the individual and the collective; Nin's
personal determination to live and to create art contrasted to the
struggle of Spain to free herself from political and economic tyranny; the undercurrent of the alliances and misalliances that were
to lead to World War II. Nin must free herself from the brief appeal
of psychoanalysis as a profession. Her combination of perceptivity
and generosity, the great influence on her own life of psychoanalysis,
naturally drew her to this work. But her cherished image of herself as a writer was stronger, and after a short time she gave up her
job assisting Rank with his patients. Although the diarist often expresses depression and even a sense of defeat, the reader is always
aware of her tenacious commitment to survival and growth.

Outwardly Anaïs Nin's life does not change very much from
1934 to 1939. She is intensely involved in literary friendships not
only with Miller but also with Lawrence Durrell, who encourages
her to create a specifically "feminine" book. She begins to collect
numerous "children," Carteret, Moricand, Gonzalo and Helba; and
the reader feels alarmed as this generous woman lends her strength
to others, giving away more and more vital power until she col-
lapses; she requires a blood transfusion to recover. Reminding one
of the conclusion of Diary I, the second Diary contains near the
end revealing remarks about a child conceived but not to be born.
At this time Nin is writing about the abortion depicted in "The
Mouse." In both cases, a new life is thwarted; the promised growth

does not occur. An overall sense of deflation is conveyed by the strong contrast between the opening and concluding sections of Diary II. The beginning in New York is dynamic, quick, exhilarating, brisk with hope. At the end, though, war has begun, and Nin must leave France and her friends to face danger and the threat of death. She returns to America in an understandably somber mood, the more so since this is Nin's second exile from her country of birth. "It was the end," she wrote, "of our romantic life." The tone, the mood, suggest irresolution. Nin and most of her children do survive numerous dangers, but during these years none succeeds in fully transcending obstacles to the full expression of life that they seek.

The bright and glowing area of Diary II is an important journey to a source of artistic inspiration and personal renewal. This is the trip to Morocco that Nin describes in pages seventy-one to seventy-nine. Her language becomes brilliantly painted and pungent with odors, everything animated by her joy of discovery and fascination with the strange. The city of Fez especially attracted the author: "Fez. One always, sooner or later, comes upon a city which is an image of one's inner cities. Fez is an image of my inner self." This insight (incidentally alluding to the future choice of the title "Cities of the Interior") was to expand in associations, burgeoning in the dark of Nin's unconscious mind. Eventually, Fez becomes identified with the womb. It is regarded as the site of woman's circuitous, mysterious, intuitive sensibility. A manifestation in the world of woman's nature, Fez suggests how that nature can find expression in writing. Nin's own "feminine" diary is a labyrinth to her, evoking the narrow twisting streets of the Moroccan city. In 1939 Nin was not yet an artist nor was she yet a free woman, but growth was taking place; her ideas about the self, the dream, and the creative process were developing. The breakthrough is to be found in her statement about the nature of woman's writing and why it is different from man's. Conversations with Miller, Durrell, and his wife Nancy served as stimulants, often as barbs, and in the process of defending her ideas about the primacy of the personal relationship to all things, Nin burst forth with an articulate formulation of the goals that she was to adopt with growing assurance during the later decades of her career. "Woman must not fabricate. She must descend into the real womb and expose its secrets and its labyrinths. She must describe it as the city of Fez, with its Arabian Nights gentleness, tranquility and mystery."[14]

This brave assertion of the mission of the woman writer was the brainchild of a woman who had yet to struggle for at least another five years before she could feel herself capable of fully assuming her life as an artist. Diaries III and IV, 1939 to 1947, describe Nin's second enforced removal from France to the United States against the background of her continued war with herself and her absorption in the lives of a host of personages who were part of the cultural life of New York City. These include the editor Dorothy Norman, Caresse Crosby, a founder with her husband of the Black Sun Press; Sherwood Anderson, the Salvador Dalis, Edgar and Louise Varèse, Richard Wright, Tennessee Williams, Louise Rainer, Canada Lee, the poets Robert Duncan, Kenneth Patchen, John Dudley, George Barker, and such figures from the art world as Noguchi, William Hayter, Ian Hugo, Leonora Carrington, Lawrence Vail, Lipchitz. Some were met only once, others a few times, while still others, especially the poets, became Nin's special friends in a city that seemed to her hypocritical (because of the constant boasting about democracy in the midst of obvious prejudice), as well as materialistic, and openly hostile to the artist. Nin wrote that America "murders" writers.[15] She tried to protect herself from the destructive New York environment by building a private world populated by her own special friends.

The theme of Diary III is loss. Again and again Nin laments the loss of Europe, its friendliness toward artists, the sense of camaraderie found in the busy yet relaxed cafes, the acceptance of the life of the senses, compared to the fear and disapproval of the Americans, among whom there are still "real dogmatic Puritans . . . a type as definite, as fanatic as the religious men of India."[16] Always yearning for her old friends, Nin devoted these first years after her arrival in New York to their re-creation in the portraits of Conrad Moricand, Jean Carteret, Hans Reichel, and the others that are collected in *Under a Glass Bell*. The tie with Henry Miller was still strong, as Nin devoted herself to writing amazing amounts of pornography in order to raise money to keep her "family" together.

This family demanded too much of its maternal center, however. Increasingly, her "children" alienated Nin with their disregard of her needs. Miller was taking the money she earned from the cheap writing that took her away from her own creative work. Duncan and Dudley, too, asked for money. She was at first puzzled and later angry when she understood that those whom she had nourished had no intention of returning what they received. "I believe the maternal in me, the mother, has been properly devoured, to the last bit, and she is dead."[17] Nin's rebellion was only secondarily against her "children"; primarily, it was against her own seemingly uncontrollable drive to protect and nurture others. The result was the breakdown that has already been discussed in these pages.

The third of Nin's published Diaries concludes after healing is underway; it closes with a sense of quiet, understated happiness that contrasts to the beginning paragraphs focused on the somber atmosphere of Paris preparing for war and the enforced separations from friends in France. Nin has had a personal triumph. She has brought together the two projects of her creative life, diary and novel. She has had a critical triumph as well. With her partner Gonzalo More at Gemor Press Anaïs Nin printed *Winter of Artifice* in 1942, and in 1944 *Under a Glass Bell*. Edmund Wilson's review in *The New Yorker* of April 1st brought Nin her first critical recognition in the United States. The journeys of the earlier volumes are here replaced by the speculative journey inward as Nin gradually defines for herself the reasons it had been so difficult for her to place her writing at the center of her life. In these pages the reader participates, becomes impatient, and occasionally wants to shake the author because of her excessive generosity. But finally he shares Nin's growth into her new sense of herself as a writer.

Diary IV is the story of the writer's emergence into public life. At Gemor Press Nin and Gonzalo printed *This Hunger* (now the first part of *Ladders to Fire*). *Ladders to Fire* was itself published in October 1946 by Dutton, and even though it did not sell well,

Dutton agreed to bring out *Children of the Albatross* without the two-year delay the publisher had originally insisted upon. "Stella" was published in *Harper's Bazaar* in 1946, its appearance there giving "an illusion of success in the world." But Nin's real success at this time was not a public one. Reviews of her books revealed an abyss between American literary expectations and the philosophy of writing that Nin was in the process of developing. The great growth that animates Diary IV is found in Nin's speculations about the arts, their interconnections, and their influence on her own style and approach to literary structure. In the 1940s Nin's Diary began to become, in part, a meditation on literature. Meanwhile, the style of the diary adapted subtly to the new emphasis on ideas; there are fewer passages of self-analysis and many more brief essays on writing, literature, and the other arts.

Diary IV is populated with creative people, not celebrities but the young writers, dancers, and musicians with whom Nin identified in her sense of exclusion from the New York literary establishment. There are names and names, and many marvelous portraits. Social activity infuses the book with a gaiety that contrasts to the sorrow of the earlier volumes. In spite of her disappointing reviews and the unenthusiastic attitude of her publisher, Nin's confidence was growing. It was nourished by her increasing depth and fluency as a writer and the encouragement and admiration of her many friends.

Still the reader is warned: "The story of complete freedom does not appear yet in this volume. I am still in the labyrinth and I must be willing to get lost before I am saved . . . Who knows what shadows from the past dictated to Edmund Wilson his next attraction? The hero of this book is the malady which makes our lives a drama of compulsion instead of freedom." The life Nin led at this time provides the background for *Children of the Albatross;* it probes the conflict of the woman who is drawn to younger men, frequently homosexual men, men who cannot be expected to fulfill her desires as a woman. Edmund Wilson, an important influence in bringing recognition to Nin's books, appears as a ghost from the past, one of those wise older men whom Nin so needed in the 1930s. As this former problem reappears, Nin is briefly drawn to Wilson, then squarely confronts her need to flee. It was not Wilson's personal qualities that threatened her but his type—that of patriarch. "With Wilson it was a matter of bowing to a new regimen, or else seducing, so as to avoid being dominated or overwhelmed or enslaved. Under cover of seduction, one avoids being controlled, influenced, possessed. For this man of power—the father—once overwhelmed me, enslaved me, dominated my life, exerted tyranny, and then betrayed me. . . . In this father-figure presence, though I am now a woman, I do not feel free or equal, able to continue my growth, my explorations, experiments, adventures. Rather I feel an apprehension that, taking my life in his hands, he may damage me. Impede me, oppress me."[18]

With this understanding, Nin passed the test. She did not become involved in a relationship that seemed so dangerous to her independence. In another sense, though, she was "still in the labyrinth." The men who had become her companions in writing—James Merrill, Paul Mathiesen, Leonard, Kendall, Laurence—inevitably disappointed and alienated her: "They bring their gaiety, their brilliance, their gifts, their charm, their beauty, and it is a magic circle. Subtly, they keep Man away, by either parody, mockery, or direct jealousy. They appropriated me." Nin reveals that "my first love was a homosexual. If his desires went to men, his poems, flowers, homages, dreams came to me." She gives us this insight into her attraction to the "luminous" children. Here is the desire to recapture the first love, so natural in one of romantic temperament. Besides this appeal, there is the sense of identity with the wounded adolescent which Nin perceived in her homosexual friends: "Something about the psyche as crippled as I was by my father's desertion, something creating difficulty in developing, in assurance, in maturing."[19]

Near its conclusion Diary IV suddenly opens into the vista of a journey. Its author has grown. She has begun to think deeply about writing. She has resisted the neurotic lure of involvement with the sort of man she knows is bad for her. She is beginning to see through the "transparent" children and to understand how they exclude her. In 1947 she began to explore ways of escaping from New

York: back to France, to Canada or to Mexico. An automobile trip across the United States initiated a new phase in her life, bringing her all the way across the country in a series of visits: to the romantic house of Weeks Hall; to Frieda Lawrence in Taos, New Mexico; to the architect Lloyd Wright and his wife Helen; to George Leite in Berkeley; and most inspiring and joyous of all to Varda himself. "Magic must predominate. Varda's attitude in life was that of a Merlin, the enchanter . . ."[20]

The journey to California circles back to the starting point of the published Diaries, for Nin is reunited with Henry Miller at his home in the Big Sur. This is where Nin's writing career began—with the friendship that developed when Miller responded to her gift of a copy of her book on Lawrence. But now their friendship seems to belong to the past. Their growth as individuals has not brought them closer. It is now Varda who represents the artist-hero. Brilliant sunlight seems to permeate the new life that Anaïs Nin embarks upon after her journey to Mexico. The harsh dark life in New York vanishes. Mexico is an atmosphere of happy, relaxed sensuousness; it invites a belief that anything is possible, even a breaking of the old designs that have constrained her:

> And one day will I open my eyes in this beautiful overwhelming place and see that I am caught in the same pattern, repeating the same story?

> How could it be otherwise? The design comes from within. It is internal.

> And yet, the next morning, swimming in the tropical sea, listening to the guitar playing and the singers on the beach, eating the freshly caught fish, drinking coconut milk from a shell, looking at the conch shells brought in by the beach boys, lying in the sun. I remembered that the definition of *tropic* was "turning," "changing," and I felt a new woman would be born here.[21]

The brilliant gold face on the jacket of the fifth Diary announces a rebirth. This is the presence, now vivid and magnificently self-confident, of the writer as a woman, for the emphasis of the fifth book reverses that of the third and fourth to bring us into the evolving consciousness, the newly asserted physical life of the woman. It seems that Anaïs Nin, having achieved her confidence as a writer, returns during the phase from 1948 to 1955 to balance her developing powers as artist with a renewal of sensuous femininity. As we have come to expect, there is discretion; but the new mood of joy suggests a personal life rich with the intimacies and vital connections that Nin so treasures. The mood of Diary V is a glow, a high: it is a time of release found in repeated trips to Mexico (and one experience with LSD); these brighten the gloom of New York City, always so oppressive and discouraging to Nin.

By 1948 the writer Nin has begun to emerge more fully into the public eye. She is very sure of her values in art, more and more involved with music and its power to heighten the art of poets ("aviators of language," she calls them here), fully committed to her own sense of style and structure; she is a mature artist now; she is filled with a self-confidence that expresses itself much more forcefully than in preceding volumes in her debates with editors and agents but especially with a new friend, the critic Maxwell Geismar. During this period Nin completes *The Four-Chambered Heart, A Spy in the House of Love,* and *Solar Barque* (which later becomes part of *Seduction of the Minotaur*.) Diary V also contains the characters and incidents that are the raw materials of *Seduction* and of *Collages*. It is a rich volume.

Nin's inner assurance is not, however, matched by the public's reaction to her books. Causing her much disappointment and occasional bitterness are uncomprehending reviews, sometimes from people whose understanding she had counted on, and the wary attitude of her publishers. While acknowledging the perfection of her style in *Spy,* editors rejected the book again and again partly for reasons of prudery and partly because of its "unreal" nature as evidenced primarily in the presence of the lie detector. The difficulty of publishing this novel caused Nin to descend occasionally to despair: "The fact I cannot face is that I am a failure as a writer. The publishers won't publish me, the bookshops won't carry my books, the critics won't write about me. I am excluded from all anthologies, and completely neglected."[22]

There is much in Nin's life to neutralize these moods: the frequent trips to Mexico, her new way of dividing her life between California and New York City; and her various friendships with creative people: Cornelia Runyon, the sculptor; the actor Reginald Pole; musicians Louis and Bebe Barron; the Ruggles; the Geismars; and the endearingly outspoken composer and critic Peggy Glanville-Hicks. The richest friendship of this period is with the writer James Leo Herlihy whom Nin met on a visit to Black Mountain College. Nin and Herlihy support each other's writing projects, exchange diaries and provide each other with inspiration and encouragement. So important was this to Nin that, besides reprinting a long passage from Herlihy's diary in Volume V, she proclaims, "He is my only link with the future."[23]

Intermingled with the joyous mood of Diary V is a quiet sadness in the form of a new recognition; it is death that Nin admits to her writing at this time: the death of Dr. Hernandez in *Seduction of the Minotaur;* in her *Diary* the deaths, first, of her father, then of her mother. While the father dominated the earlier Diaries, Nin's mother is the central figure here, for through her analysis with Inge Bogner Nin came gradually to accept the parts of herself that most closely resembled those of her mother, a severe and often angry woman whose most appealing feature was a lovely singing voice. Speculating that she may have lost her mother's love with her rebellion against the Catholic Church at age sixteen, Nin is now mature enough to understand how deeply her own intense identification with her father must have hurt Rosa Culmell. "But some bonds are never broken. I inherited from my mother not only her gold thimble, a sewing machine, but the maternal passion and care for others."[24]

The air of gentle acceptance that pervades *Diary V* softens the moments of grief as they are not softened in earlier volumes. If New York presents a competitive and hostile atmosphere, one can fly away to California or to Mexico into the sunlight and leisurely rhythms of a people who enjoy life in an undemanding way, finding happiness in the routines of their lazy days and absorbing the healing sunlight along with the smells of hotly seasoned food and the cleansing splash of the sea on the body. The several Mexican journeys of Diary V sustain Nin's gaiety and make possible a tolerance for disappointment. She returns to Paris, apprehensive lest she find that everything has changed for the worse, as she has been warned. And there is, in fact, a melancholy about this return to a place once so beloved; the reader does feel Paris has changed, but Nin does not. She rediscovers what she seeks. She sees Paris with the eyes of a lover and she departs contented.

Diary V, finally, is a success story. Privileged to share the life of a woman who is determined to seek her own evolution, the reader also shares her success. Nin is not yet well-known when Diary V closes; she has attained a limited if very enthusiastic recognition as a writer, but she has not sacrificed any part of her integrity in the struggle. On the contrary, the woman has grown with the artist. The presence of this woman, at once fragile and hardy, flows through Diary V with the serenity of maturity. This book is a tribute to tenacity. The success it depicts is entirely free from materialism or the desire to interpret one's success as a proof of superiority over others. A spiritual quality manifests itself in the pages of Diary V. There is an acceptance of a destiny that is very far indeed from a narrow concern with self. "During the music I meditated on my personal death. I realized I must complete my work, because I am an instrument for human consciousness and an instrument constantly disciplined to create . . ."[25]

The sixth volume of the Diary brings Nin the realization of a cherished dream: the publication of Diary I. It is this triumph which brings to a close the large volume that spans the decade from 1955 to 1966. Diary VI is strikingly different from its predecessors. Nin herself is now firmly established in the realm of the external. She is a mature artist with a total view of reality and of people that is a contrast to the delicate, tentative, evanescent feelings of the earlier volumes. Diary V glows with an aura of the sensuous. Diary VI is sometimes almost crisp. The decade that Nin recreates as she weaves her very full life between California and New York is itself a drab time, a period of national reticence, of conservative, even reactionary, policies and attitudes. Nin herself now seems to be a part of the U.S. Yet she is still incurably, and understandably, homesick for France.[26]

In Diary VI the emphasis shifts from Anaïs, the woman who struggles to maintain her image as an artist, to the culture in which her battle for recognition is taking place. Volume VI is more nearly historical than any of the earlier volumes. With great skill Nin evokes the painting and sculpture exhibits and the concerts she attends on both coasts. She describes numerous trips to Europe, one to Sweden, where she was very warmly received, and several flights to France, which brought her the joy of "reconnection."[27] There is a happy reunion with Henry Miller, and there are dozens of portraits of creative people. To mention only a few: Romain Gary; Lesley Blanch; Allan Ginsberg; the Huxleys; Julian Beck and Judith Malina; Edgar and Louise Varèse; Tennessee Williams; the always-engaging Caresse Crosby; Kim Stanley; and, of course, James Leo Herlihy, whose friendship continues to provide Nin with the intellectual exchange and emotional support of a loving confidant.

The publisher Alan Swallow is portrayed as a generous and sensible man who performed a valuable service by printing the "specialized" books of writers like Nin. Swallow represents himself admirably in his letters to Nin, which communicate a great intelligence and a devotion to good writing. It is pleasant to meet the ebullient Varda once again. He is marvelous as the author of his autobiography.[28] Another of Nin's many faces is revealed in Diary VI. She becomes active as a critic of the arts.[29] Lengthy sections of the sixth volume contain her reviews of and personal responses to books, films, and art exhibits. There is reticent and balanced praise for Ginsberg's *Howl.* There is enthusiastic praise for the fiction of Robert Lindner, of Anna Kavan, and, of course, for Lawrence Durrell's *Justine,* which Nin greeted joyously as the beginning of a return to an appreciation of poetic prose.

During these years Nin the writer is enormously concerned with the two related problems of editing and publishing the Diary; and the great topic that began to occupy the attention of people in the 1960s;

the use of drugs to achieve expanded consciousness. An always thoughtful and sometimes impassioned debate about the benefits and the dangers of LSD takes up many pages of Diary VI. Nin was tempted to believe that the widespread use of LSD could inspire a swift revolution of consciousness. But this hope was countered by her own experience with the drug; its use was accompanied by physical illness; and, second, Nin did not attain levels of awareness that she could not attain without LSD. In *The Novel of the Future,* which Nin wrote after the years encompassed by Diary VI, she makes clear her position against the use of LSD and other hallucinogens. Yet in the late fifties and early sixties the transformative possibilities of LSD captivated her imagination. When Richard Alpert told her that he understood her books for the first time after taking LSD, Nin exclaimed, with typical humor: "Would I have to pack LSD with each book?"[30]

Although the emphasis of Diary VI is on the outer life, the personal theme is always present, and the great concern in both spheres is transformation. As always psychoanalysis is Nin's personal faith and her means of achieving the transformations she desires in her personal life. And during the period chronicled in Diary VI the enemy that Nin had constantly to combat was the bitterness she felt at being overlooked by the literary establishment of the U.S. By 1955 Nin learned to value her own work, but the public and the critics had not nor had the editors who might have published it, with the exception of Alan Swallow. Naturally, the success of a facile book like *Bonjour Tristesse* would cause pain to a writer of Nin's psychological depth and technical sophistication. Nin understood that one reason U.S. audiences reacted favorably to such a highly intellectual work as *Waiting for Godot* was "because the dreamer and the madman have smelly feet." Sensitive to the effect bitterness would have on her own life and writing, Nin resisted it. To the correspondent who is called "poet in prison," she wrote: "Bitterness is the thing to watch—toxic. I watch it in myself; when I see it growing like an abscess, I operate fast."[31] The operations were successful. The continual effort to concentrate on the positive aspects of her experience brought Nin intimate friendships with

writers who, like herself, have had to fight for acceptance: William
Goyen; Maude Hutchins; and, most important, Marguerite Young,
the author of *Miss Macintosh, My Darling*. Miss Young is the artist
heroine of Diary VI. A mutual love of fantasy, of the imaginative
in art, a passion for language, a tenderness toward the neglected
and the unloved drew Nin and Young into a deep, sustaining friendship. The strongest proof of Nin's resistance to bitterness is the remarkable generosity she has always shown toward other writers, a
generosity that increased during these years when Nin's own work
was not receiving much attention. Nin's praise of *Miss Macintosh*
is a beautiful tribute.[32]

The most important "action" of Diary VI is the publication
(thanks to Alan Swallow's interest and efforts) of the first volume of
the Diary. This caused Nin intense ambivalence. She wanted to
publish it even more fervently than when she first began showing it
to editors in the 1930s. Although Nin still wanted to use the journal
as a source for fiction, she was working hard to transform the
journal into art. She worried: "I sometimes have the feeling that
my diary is not a finished work and needs filling." She wondered
whether the Diary ought to have "a climax, as in a novel." Then,
with a note of triumph, she wrote: "I seem to know at last how to
handle the diary. After the diary is written roughly like a sketchbook, there has to be a craft like that of the fiction writer in the
choice and cutting." At the same time she was engaged in this task
of transformation, Nin began to question her own adherence to the
perspective of the personal. Again, there is ambivalence. Nin identified her own art with that of Marguerite Young, which she praised,
writing that Young "englobed." Nin said: "The female need to
nourish, to encompass, to hold, commune with, was fulfilled in the
spider-like web [of *Miss Macintosh, My Darling*]. Thus was life
contained, no intellectual invention like Joyce's, every beginning
taken from life and then magnified, expanded, but rooted in some
natural seed." Nin stood by the concept of the "feminine" in writing that is contained in the pages of Diary II. The connection between life and art must be maintained; woman's art is more likely
than man's to perform this service. "Long ago Otto Rank, who had

written so much about the artist, stated that woman had not created imaginative works such as *Don Quixote* or *Ulysses* because she feared to cut the umbilical cord, to separate from the human and the personal. I had this fear. Out of it was born the diary."[33]

In spite of this affirmation of her personal esthetic and of the work that had evolved from it, Nin had two problems with regard to the Diary. For the first time (as far as one can judge from the published Diaries) she began to doubt the efficacy, the completeness, of her devotion to the principle of intimacy and personalization. An evening spent with people who talked about Artaud from an intellectual point of view made Nin wonder whether in the Diary she had "sacrificed objective knowledge." She wrote in a rare mood of "condemnation" of the Diary. Nin decided to try to "see people from all angles," to include "objective" views of the people she was writing about with the personal "subjective" ones. As always with Nin, a sense of inadequacy was quickly translated into a new aspiration.[34]

But the conflict remained. The desire to publish the Diary was powerful. The desire to conceal it, to protect it, to continue to nurture the Diary in darkness was also powerful. Nin has often said that her "demons" are in the Diary. Twice in the pages of Diary VI Nin recorded an urge to burn the Diary. To publish it was to give birth, to relinquish the growth inside, to allow her creation to enter the world and to meet its fate. Not only the creation but also its creator would be judged. For a time Nin drew back. In the summer of 1965 she wrote: "Suddenly it seemed to me I was exposing myself to the maliciousness of the world. No. I would not publish it."[35]

But, of course, she did. Working with Dr. Bogner, Nin resolved this excruciating conflict. It is not surprising that Nin's fear took the form of a nightmare. She dreamed that she opened her front door and was struck by "mortal" radiation.[36] This dream seems prophetic. The publication of the Diary did, in fact, change Nin's life almost violently, but in a very beautiful and positive way. She attained the sense of connection with the world that she had longed for since childhood. Nin became a public figure, the unofficial spokeswoman for thousands of other women, the representative, as well, of the artist and of all those "sensitive Americans" to whom *The Novel of the Future* was later to be dedicated.

To read Diary VI, which spans a decade ending in 1966, is a strange experience in which there is a measure of dramatic irony. Today we know what Nin did not know when she concluded her Diary entries for 1966: that she achieved recognition and fame; that she established an exchange of feelings and ideas with the world; that she was intensely involved in the process of transforming the cultural values of the U.S.; and that she was moving closer and closer to achieving her proper evaluation and respect as an artist. Although Volume VII of the Diary is not yet in print, the recent collections *A Woman Speaks* and *In Favor of the Sensitive Man* give a full portrait of the Anaïs Nin who emerged into public life after the Diaries began to appear in 1966. The woman who spoke in the 1970s was a gayer, happier, more powerful, and more fulfilled woman than the one we met in the Diaries of the earlier years. The woman herself was a tribute to her own steady belief in growth and in maturity.

It is an irony worth noting that Nin achieved fame in the culture in which she had felt uneasy for decades, and which she had frequently criticized for its insensitivity and its neglect of the artist. The explanation of this irony is not simple. It is partly that there actually *is* a subtle and gradual transformation of values occurring (to some extent as a result of Nin's influence); but it is also partly because Nin herself fit into the tradition of the popular American myth of the person who, without many advantages, "makes good" by virtue of persistence and hard work. Nin has often said that her "genius" is really a quality of tenacity. She was persistent in developing her talent, in combating her own self-defeating feelings and actions; in fighting illness; in maintaining artistic integrity against the pressure of more or less steady critical disdain; in sustaining a faith in the future of serious writing in this country (a faith that is more and more difficult for writers to sustain); and in her devotion to her friends and fellow writers. Nin's commonsense and her generosity are always evident. In 1961, writing to James Leo Herlihy, she announced:

I have given up novel writing. I have decided to enjoy what I have, typing out the diaries for the far-off future, stacking wood, enjoying sunsets and martinis, and forget I am a writer. When I was nine years old I had decided to live for others, and I should have stuck to my decision. But do tell me all the good things that your success has brought you, your pleasures, because as I say, they balance in the books of the mystics.[37]

The "Journal des Autres"

> I can easily believe in the disintegration of the body, but cannot believe that all I have learned, experienced, accumulated, can disappear and be wasted. Like a river, it must flow somewhere. Proust's life flowed into me, became a part of my life. His thoughts, his discoveries, his visions, each year visit me, each year bring me deeper messages. There must be continuity. The mockingbirds of California sing intermittently but sumptuously.
>
> —*The Diary of Anaïs Nin, Volume V*

The literary work that Nin's Diary most closely resembles is Proust's *roman-fleuve,* the great masterpiece of autobiograpical fiction, *A la recherche du temps perdu.* This is both because of a profound affinity between the two authors and because of direct influence.[1] For Nin the "three gods of the deep" are Dostoevski, Lawrence, and Proust. Of these three, only Lawrence and Proust have had a profound and lasting influence on Nin's writing, and that of Proust has been more profound and longer lasting than that of Lawrence. The French author has provided Nin not only with a model of literary achievement that manifests the qualities she strives for in her own work, but also because the man himself is a fascinating figure of the artist, a hero for Nin to add (with important reservations) to her pantheon of creators. Nin's non-fiction is filled with references to Proust. His name is mentioned on the first page of Diary I. The Diaries contain over one hundred references to Proust and his work. There are twenty-five more in *The Novel of the Future* and more still in the published speeches and essays.[2] She quotes from Proust's work. She cites passages from Leon Pierre Quint's book on Proust. All but about ten of these references express admiration and love. Nin reread *Remembrance of Things Past* once a year. Quite simply, Proust is her favorite writer.

142

Again and again Nin records in her Diary what she has learned or wishes to learn from Proust. She is impressed by the depth of his characterizations: "Keep my aim in sight. I have a very big, impersonal aim: to impart the discoveries I have made about character. I write about uncommon characters so that we may become them. Proust solved this. He wrote in depth about characters who did not have any depth. His characters swim in his own unconscious. They are ordinary people but Proust looked beyond them and at a collective depth and made profound deductions." Proust's style is praised in a sentence that is worth quoting for its beauty: "the sea-sound of Proust's phrases echo through the marvelous eternal edifice of his lucidities." Nin especially admires the French novelist's ability to evoke delicate states of awareness, the fragile states of semi-consciousness that she calls the "half-dream."[3]

Proust's use of his own life to create the *Remembrance* gave Nin a magnificent example of what can be created in art by a sensitive and thorough exploitation of one's self. She contemplates Proust's example: "Every now and then I feel I should transform the diary, as Proust did in his life and memories." More than a decade later, she writes: "I don't know why I can't give the diary the continuity and unity of a Proustian work." (This is an ironic comment for Nin *has* achieved the continuity and unity of a Proustian work.) The flowing nature of Proust's structure attracted Nin, who has sought just such an organic structure both for her fiction and for her Diary. She calls the *Remembrance* "an unbroken web." She compares it to the endless scarf as a metaphor for a book (the dream of Nin's novelist friend, Marguerite Young). Moreover, Nin has always understood that Proust was not at all adrift in the stream-of-consciousness, but was, as she herself is, particularly in the Diaries, an historical writer, a chronicler of the social and cultural life of specific times and of specific places. Nin has defended Proust's power of realism for she sees that his vision, like her own, is comprehensive: an art of surfaces and of depths projected simultaneously within a flowing structure.[4]

The richness of meaning that Proust holds for Nin has been steady through the years and quite consistent. Yet there has been an observable process of evolution. During the period of Diary I, partly because Nin was living in France, she felt close to Proust. She introduced Miller to the French author and there ensued a dialogue about love, especially Proust's handling of the affair between Marcel and Albertine. At this time Nin perceived, but did not focus upon, a facet of Proust's art that was later to become central: the way in which feeling instead of chronology endows time with significant patterns. This was disclosed by the process of free association in her therapy with Rank, but Nin noted that the Proustian view of time was similar to the psychoanalytical: ". . . these talks follow a capricious, associative pattern which is elusive. The order made in reality, chronological, is another matter entirely. Rank does not believe in that 'construction' by logic and reason. The truth lies elsewhere. In what one connects to one's self, by emotion (as in Proust). I began to perceive a new order which lies in the choice of events made by memory. This selection is made by the power of the emotion. No more calendars!"[5]

The second Diary reveals a different aspect of Nin's relationship to Proust: that is, her ambivalence about making an emotional identification with the man as an artist. She is both attracted and repelled by Proust's withdrawal from life and his suffering. When Henry refers to her fear of change as Nin's "malady," she retorts: " 'Well, if it is my malady, Henry, I should express it to the utmost through the diary, make something of the diary, just as Proust made his work out of his disease. . . .' " And later, when she felt overwhelmed by the demands of her friends, Nin wrote: "Like Proust, I shall have to manufacture some handicap so as to be able to write instead of being consumed." The process of moving nearer to a total identification with Proust was a gradual one. Besides being complicated by his example of neurosis and suffering (an example which Nin eventually repudiated), she was naturally uncomfortable because Proust was a male. The mature Nin is serene with this difference of gender, but it was disturbing to her during the years of *Diary II,* when Nin had very little confidence in the power of women as artists. Male artists seemed capable of achieving heights forever impossible to female artists: "Woman is more alone than man. She cannot find the 'eternal moments' in art as man does, as Proust did, even if she is an artist." Caught between the (false) alternatives of art or life, Nin—for a time—felt obliged to choose life; femininity (at this time she thought of novel-writing as "masculine"); and the diary (a "feminine" form of writing): "I must go the opposite way from Proust who found eternal moments in creation. I must find them in life."[6]

This conflict was profound, for Nin did want to be like Proust, the artist, just as she wanted to identify with her father, the artist. The struggle is described primarily in Diary II. Flattered by Stuart Gilbert's having told her that she had "the makings of a Proust," Nin attempted to gain strength from the comparison. She expressed pride in her "X-ray vision," so like that of the French novelist, and she defended the Proustian type of symbolism against Henry's attacks. Eventually, Nin's conflict about Proust produced very positive results in the form of a fundamental insight and an embrace of a faith: "This for me is the labyrinth. Identification, projection. . . . Is it this deep psychological truth I will explore to the limit, and make the base of my Proustian edifice? It is at the basis of my life, analogy, interchange of souls, of identities. Doesn't love mean just that, this growing into the other like plants intertwining their roots, this interchange of soul and feelings. Not an abyss then, but a new world. Not madness but a deep truth. A principle moving us, our inner fatality. We do not act as ourselves. We act. We are possessed. These are the multiple miracles of the personality."[7]

Proust has been Nin's guide through the labyrinth of identifications and projections on which rests her entire body of work. The reader can trace her circuitous journey through the pages of the third, fourth, and fifth Diaries and arrive at a point of intimacy and love in the pages of the sixth Diary. Upon meeting the son of friends, Nin noted that had she and Proust had a son, he would have resembled this particular young man, a reflection that gives support to the idea that Proust has served Nin not only as literary exemplar but also, and perhaps more significantly, as a muse. As a mature woman, Nin became as excited as a child when sitting against a wall on the other side of which were Proust's notebooks.

The identification she made between his work and her work provided consolation during moments of depression: "My Proustian world is my only joy, tracing webs and correlations." In Diary II Nin lamented: "I do feel I have something to accomplish, a destiny to fulfill, but, like Proust, I am not sure that what I am doing is important." But by 1965 Nin's identity as writer was so strong and so unassailable that she was able to proclaim: "I feel like Proust, that I must get the diary done before I die. . . ."[8]

In Anaïs Nin's *oeuvre* there are two "Proustian edifices": the fiction and the Diary. Both are highly individual works, ingenious and powerful, and both are finely poised between autobiography and fiction. However, because the Diary retains and even emphasizes the historical dimension that has been suppressed in the fiction, it is the Diary that more nearly resembles the *Recherche du temps perdu*.

In both cases the exact line between fiction and fact is impossible to draw without the assistance of a literary historian; but in neither case is this demarcation particularly important. Consciousness does not observe the distinction between fact and fantasy until it has been trained to do so. With most novelists it is impossible to know how much of the imaginary has gone into a novel or how much heightening the "real" has received; this is partly because we have no access to the process of creation unless the writer has kept notebooks or journals which have been made available to the public. Nin is an exception. In her Diary we can see just exactly how her fiction has been "distilled," as she says, from the ongoing record of her life. We can see how she has made a drama of consciousness by giving continuity to what she has experienced through the interpretations of the self that re-creates, then analyzes its own experiences. Perhaps the most fascinating of these are the experiences of consciousness itself. In the work of Proust and Nin alike the reader shares in the process by means of which consciousness, with its multifaceted powers and its capacity to meditate upon itself, creates works of art from its own resources. At the center of *Cities of the Interior* as well as the Diary is the comprehensive, all-seeing, all-knowing "I." The analogy to Proust, once again, seems a natural one: "The

Diary was held together," Nin wrote, "was given its unity by my being at the center. The novels? In whose consciousness does the whole appear? Shall I be there as Proust was, but invisible as a catalyzer?"[9]

Like Proust's narrator Marcel, the "I" of Nin's Diary uses the act of writing to preserve and to protect experience in the very process of interpreting this experience. Through writing, the once frivolous Marcel gains a sense of worth that redeems the time he had wasted in the past. Marcel discovers how he can employ his memories to recover the past he has seemingly lost during the course of a pleasant but superficial life. Through the act of writing he is rescued from the meaninglessness of this life; through art he regains not only his self-esteem but also the past time that only seems to have disappeared. This is his great discovery. Association is the nature of the process that frees him from the prison of time and enables him to embark upon his journey backward into what has already happened, though not in the same way since he who experiences it has changed and is no longer exactly the same man who *had* experienced this life. As time, seemingly, moves forward, carrying his individual life toward its end, Marcel moves backward in countermovement, defiantly, at once recapturing the past and reliving his life in a retrogression from age toward youth. It is the power of memory that makes this triumph possible. Nin, however, lacks her mentor's trust in the unpredictable meandering path of memory. Memory threatens her with its unreliability: "Memory is a great betrayer. Whenever I read it [the Diary], I find it differs from the way I remembered the scenes and the talk. I find scenes I had forgotten, thoughts I had forgotten, and precisions noted at the time have become foggy or vanish altogether." Since Nin's effort is one of protection of experience, almost primitively, as a part of herself, she has been determined not to let time rob her of anything: "Over and over again I discover the diary is an effort against loss, the passing, the deaths, the uprootings, the witherings, the unrealities. I feel that when I enclose something, I save it. It is alive here. When anyone left, I felt I retained his presence in these pages."[10]

From Proust Nin learned to trust her interpretations of her experience, to accept its legitimacy as the material of art, and to reject invention in a spirit of loyalty to the personal observations and experiences to which alone one can feel a strong and immediate relation. Far from being reportorial autobiographies, *Remembrance of Things Past* and Nin's Diary are creations that arise from meticulously observed and carefully preserved materials flowing directly from the lives of unusually sensitive observers. Proust's characters and situations are disguised, sometimes thinly, as Nin's usually are not; hers have been exposed to the sharpening of a novelist's eye and pen. Both works display a remarkable trust in experience itself to create its own unity as the unpredictable trail of free association leads the relaxed observer into unexpected adventures. A delicious scent at tea time awakened Proust's awareness of the strange power of involuntary memory, elusive, resistant, impossible to summon by an act of will. For Nin it was psychology that showed the possibilities of evolving organic form by following the path of one's associations. When one creates an organic structure by lending oneself to the patterns that emerge when rational control is relaxed, the result is an easily unrolling form that invents itself as it flows from situation to situation. The pace is leisurely. There is time to spare for meditative passages, for set pieces, for comment on art and politics. Because the reader does not know what is coming next (there being no conventional plot line to give things away) and because the nature of the work seems to accommodate virtually any sort of material, the organic form employed by Proust—and natural to Nin in diary-keeping—always holds the possibility of great surprise. Who knows whom he may meet next? Where he will be transported, into which distant land, living room, studio, or café? Or which familiar friends he may meet again a volume or so hence? Anything is possible, providing it falls within the range of interests of the narrating "I."

Similar themes fascinate Nin as fascinated Marcel Proust. All radiate from the center of the "I" (eye) as it undertakes its journeys: into society; to the sea shore, the mountains, across the country; to Morocco, Mexico, to Balbec; or into unexplored realms of the self. There are the shared themes: love, disappointment in love; the subworld of homosexuals, their masks, their hidden lives; the infatuation with art, painting, with music in particular; and above all, the sensitive child's adoration of the artist. Proust's and Nin's works contain a double view: outward toward society; inward toward the self. Like Proust, Nin gives us marvelous evocations of parties, dances, conversations, a host of social gatherings. Like Proust, she has an eye for the ridiculous and a capacity for satire, but generally her compassion softens the portraits of people she dislikes. Among the best of her gently satirical scenes are the party at Caresse Crosby's home which the Salvador Dalis attended and the battle over Angelo's Cafe which Varda decorated. Nin's sense of ironic humor appears at its most subtle when the man who delivered copies of *Ladders to Fire,* asked: " 'Do you make a lot of money out of a book like that?' "; or when she tells of a woman who wanted Nin to accompany her to a house of male prostitution but was too modest to discuss her problems with a psychoanalyst. Nin's eye for this type of absurdity is sharp, but her empathy prevents her from mocking. Nin's evocations of places are as detailed and as appealing as are her portraits of the hundreds of people who appear in the pages of the Diary. When printed alone, Nin's descriptions of foreign cities and countries are self-sustaining and impressive, but they take on added vitality when read in the context of the Diary among the monochromatic scenes of Paris or New York. The contrast between the dark, competitive, often discouraging life of the cities and the buoyancy and brightness of Mexico, Morocco, or Bali is an essential aspect of the Diary's dramatic impact. The way that travel breaks the rhythm of Nin's life, giving it variety and providing periods of renewal, is an essential part of Nin's experience, and the alternating pace is a part of the Diary's underlying structure.

As in the *Remembrance,* in the Diary the structure wrought by the meditation of consciousness upon its own experience knows no boundaries; the flowing movement is a "tale without beginning or end." It is vast, capacious, and easily accommodates all that Nin responds to vividly before recounting these experiences in vivid language. Nin's Diary, like Proust's novel, is an act of devotion to art. He called his novel "a cathedral." Nin's Diary is the only sustained meditation on art that exists in the literature of the U.S. (a fact that helps explain why it has been dismissed and even ridiculed by those who speak for a culture that retains its Puritan suspicion of beauty). In Nin's and Proust's writing alike, the love of art is so fervent that it cannot be satisfied by the *act* of making a work of art, but must also—and simultaneously—comprise a meditation upon itself.

Some of the finest lyrical passages in the Diary serve to connect or reconnect emotions and art, art and the other creative acts of life. In the pages of the Diary the past is brought into the present, revitalized, re-experienced; in the Diary continuity and discontinuity are reconciled; in the Diary conflicts are resolved between life and the myth; between conscious and unconscious experience, between the "subjective" and the "objective"; between life and art—all are resolved through the use of the magic image to create unity by transcending paradox. One of Nin's most tender and haunting dreams has its source in her love of Proust. When Nin was tormented by conflicts and by indecision, she was visited by a healing vision: the window of Proust's house. (The house was identical to one in which she had lived.) Proust's window was "open on two avenues," suggesting, quite naturally, the two ways of Proust: the Guermantes Way, which leads to the past, to history, to the external life, to objectivity, to fact; and the alternate path which leads to the intimate and personal choices of love and of art, to the way of M. Swann. Proust's Marcel explores both these paths and is able to unite them in his art. Nin took from her dream the message that the "labyrinth of remembrance" provides the healing journey because from this labyrinth the artist can create "the endless book."[11]

The lessons taught by Proust are essential to the nature and the individuality of Nin's approach to writing. They are the lessons of modernism, lessons which seem to require review in the postmodern era in which we now live. We have nearly lost sight of the radical past, of the first decades of this century in which so many vital questions were raised about the nature of reality. The central issue in Nin's work, one of great complexity, is the fundamental nature of the self. This question naturally leads to others, to inquiries about how we apprehend reality; about the relationships between time and space; about what determines the experience of a human being in a world in which everything is constantly in a state of ceaseless motion and change. "Relativity" is one of the terms most frequently used by Nin in her non-fiction.

Nin has repeatedly given Proust credit for teaching her how to break down conventional chronology (this is also one of the many lessons of psychoanalysis). Often there is a time lapse between an event and the emotion that it has stimulated or inspired, as Proust shows, for example, in his treatment of Marcel's delayed grief after his grandmother's death. Naturally, when a writer abandons chronology (the arrangement of events in sequence) and chooses to portray only those moments in his characters' lives that are animated by emotion, only those moments when the characters are truly "alive," then the resulting structure may seem arbitrary even though there is a meaningful principle behind the selection of incidents. At first hidden, this structure takes its significance from the patterns displayed by the characters' emotional lives. When the reader understands this, the seeming leaps and jumps from incident to incident, character to character will form coherent patterns, for time is being measured not sequentially but by the intensity of what the characters feel. Feeling creates its own reality. "I never generalize, intellectualize," Nin has written. *"I see, I hear, I feel.* These are my primitive instruments of discovery."[12] What the alert and sensitive self discovers is emotion. Emotion personalizes both time and space.

Nin conceives of the self not as a fixed, unalterable, "given" entity but as a process, a motion toward evolution, caught up in a ceaseless state of becoming. The self is, paradoxically, immersed in the flowing of life *at the same time* that it is engaged in a theoretically unlimited process of expansion. The self experiences emotions; these emotions create connections to other people; these relationships then change the self, which becomes an altered entity, preferably an expanded one. All time zones are present simultaneously in the ongoing state of awareness that comprises the self. Nin knows that the past can never be discarded, that it is always transforming itself into and influencing what we call the present, yet her personal orientation is toward the future, which is the realm of hope, aspiration, of promise. "I seek to escape from the past," she writes; "I prefer unfamiliar landscapes, unfamiliar atmospheres. I love change of setting, futuristic designs, changes of fashion, frequent metamorphosis, shedding of the past in all its forms. After a while I discard a dress not because it is worn . . . but because the self which enjoyed that particular dress has changed, has outworn it, needs to assume another color, another shape." A devotee of motion and of change, Nin also values stability and continuity. Proust taught her the "continuity of relationships." At the same time he showed her that "a single face can wear a thousand masks, that personality is reducible to a discontinuous series of psychological states."[13]

Continuity and discontinuity. Both describe the nature of the self. The self is continuous because there is a center unique to each individual that remains stable, but not fixed, as it evolves through a lifetime. This continuity is associated with the flowing motion that Nin values so highly. At the same time, the self is discontinuous. It is formed of many parts, of discrete pieces that form patterns. These patterns shift, fall apart, and come together again to form new patterns. They are like the bits and pieces of colored glass in a kaleidoscope. The force that gives the self the impetus to form a new pattern may be a powerful experience, or it may be the impact of another person, a friend or lover. This paradox that unites continuity and discontinuity is easy to observe; it has the intuitive feeling of being an accurate description, but it is difficult to explain. The self is always changing, but it is also always the same.

Long ago Rimbaud made the mysterious statement that "Je est un autre." The self can, of course, pretend to be somebody else in the hope that the power of the performance will transform the actor into his desired image of self. As she has identified with Proust, Nin has also identified with Rimbaud. In her case, it is provocative to translate the idea of the "I" being "somebody else" into the idea of the "I" being a variety of other people. If the Diary is regarded as an extension of Nin's self, then the woman plus the Diary comprise her total self. The Diary contains and reflects all the possible selves of Anaïs Nin, or the self as well as its many masks. At the same time, it also is the "Journal des autres," as those readers who recognize themselves in its pages have always known. An extremely complex person, Nin has worn many masks, though they changed over the years from the ones adopted by the suffering young woman who appealed to her Diary in a pathetic tone: "My dear Diary, it is Anaïs who is speaking to you, and not someone who thinks as everybody should think. Dear Diary, pity me, but listen to me."[14]

A single self wears many masks, a fact that greatly complicates the attempt to define any one person's self. Adding to this complexity is the possibility that there are false as well as authentic masks. The process of socialization creates the first masks: those that people adopt for the roles they must play in life. Anaïs Nin, for example, was a dutiful daughter, a loving sister, an upper-middleclass housewife, an elegant and refined European "lady." These masks had to be torn away from the face of the woman beneath if she was to be free to express her authentic self. Nin's authentic self is rebellious, creative, and, in a positive sense, extremely willful. This self likes to defy convention, but always beautifully and tastefully, and enjoys a talent for self-dramatization. One of the most distinctive characteristics of Anaïs Nin's self is an extraordinarily sensitive and keenly developed capacity for empathy. This trait gives her strength as a writer, but at times during her life when her ego was relatively weak, this ready gift of empathy could be threatening. Sometimes, her intense sense of identification with other people tended to obliterate her sense of who she was herself: "It is as if by a fluid quality, a facility for identification with others, I became like water and instead of separating from others, as Henry does, I lose myself in others. . . . Then I get confused."[15]

However, when she could master her "confusion" and allow herself to form relationships of fusion, Nin was able to add dimensions to her self. The sentences that follow the above quotation introduce the curious notion of twinship that has played a crucial role in Nin's development, and, if Otto Rank was correct in his theory, plays a role in the growth of all people.[1] Fully to understand Rank's thought about the concept of twinship, it is necessary to read both *Art and Artist* and his book *The Double: A Psychological Study.* Various relationships offer experiences of likeness or of difference; in his writings Rank has explained why people require both

kinds of relationships in order to form and to differentiate ourselves from others. "Identification, projection. My identification
with my father which had to be broken. Myself in June. I see the
double, the twins of others." Well along in her task of disposing of
the masks that were inhibiting her self from directing her life, Nin
exclaimed: "I have no twin to my writing. It is a big burden for a
woman."[16] Twinship, as Nin explored it during several decades provided her with a process for adding four distinct types of identity to
her sense of self. There is twinship with another woman, June, for
example; there is twinship with one's brother (as in the early stories
and novellas); twinship with one's father (as explored in "Winter of
Artifice"); and, finally, there is twinship with one's fellow artist, the
relationship of the female artist to the male artist, a relationship in
which there is a symbolic exchange of "masculine" and "feminine"
qualities. Numerous men have served as muses to Nin, as she to
them. But it is Proust whose influence and example have had the
most pervasive and most powerful effect upon Nin's life and art.

When Nin was in the process of "unmasking" so as to reveal the
artist who was her self, she was critical of Proust for using the "I"
of Marcel to generalize about all people. In 1937 she wrote, "The
only flaw I find in Proust is his generalization. . . . If only Proust
had spoken for himself, without saying: 'lovers, jealousy, all sus-
picion, all lovers.'" And, again, "I should not say 'woman' and
generalize as Proust does, I should say I, Anaïs, to be more exact."
Later on this criticism was withdrawn. Nin came to understand that
the self has a collective dimension as well as an individual one, and
she grew to trust the reliability of her own self as an instrument
sufficiently sensitized to register general human conditions. She accepted the Jungian view that some dreams express the individual
part of the self, the ego, while others express the collective dimension, portraying archetypal patterns of deep universal significance.
By 1945 Nin had become confident of her capacity and of her right
to speak for woman: "I inhabit the unconscious," she wrote, "and
I will always write from that realm, deeper and deeper, until I reach
the collective unconscious of woman.[17]

There is no specific moment at which the timid woman who

longed to be a writer but devoted most of her energy to helping other writers, became Anaïs Nin the writer, whose energies were focused on her work but who did not give up her full personal life. The "I" changed and grew gradually into a strength of identity that required new, and more authentic, masks. Nin's "hidden" self emerged as the artist, the teacher, the public figure, whose role demanded calm, quietly joyous, controlled, yet humorous *personae*. As she developed, Nin did not actually shed the old masks but grew more comfortable with them. In the process, she also had the strength and the discipline to add yet more masks to her identity. As she has often said, when conflicts are resolved, energy is released. As one sees from reading the Diaries, the "I" of Anaïs Nin encompasses a strong determined center, or self, and many *personae*. The identifications that once threatened her with loss of self actually increased, becoming Nin's source of power as a writer. The woman who had criticized Proust for using the narrative "I" to generalize about the human condition grew so certain of the validity of her own perceptions that during a question-and-answer period after one of her talks, she referred to her Diary as "*our* Diary." The gradual expansion of her concept of her self to include her readers has now become complete: "I'm not worried about the metamorphosis of the diary which has now become universal, in other words, which has become *our* diary."[18]

Nin seems always to have thought of herself as a reflector for other people, but she has not always been comfortable with this function. As a very young woman she proclaimed with a note of pride: "I am like the crystal in which people find their mystic unity." But when Rank asked her why she felt she needed treatment, Nin responded: "I felt like a shattered mirror." Increasingly, with maturity and a sense of comfort with her public and private roles, Nin began to employ metaphors for the self that are nonhuman and that, typically, invoke a comparison to instruments used for reflection or to enhance vision. She argues that we must become aware of the flaws in this instrument if we are to correct defects in our vision: "The only objectivity we can reach is achieved, first of all, by an examination of our *self* as lens, as camera, as recorder, as mirror."[19]

Nin once distinguished three uses of the principle of the mirror in her work; of importance in this context is the third: "the mirror that I am in the diary when I portray others." A statement made at about the same time clarifies Nin's idea of the nature of the mirror. It is not simply a passive reflector, as the moon for the sun; the mirror has an identity of its own. The act of reflection is one of its functions. Moreover, there are different sizes of mirrors: "Of course it's necessary to be an individual, to be the proper mirror for others. If you have a small mirror you cannot reflect big personalities. In my great effort to perfect myself as a sensitive instrument with a wide range I made a comparison always to the mirror. The mirror has to have identity and an existence and intelligence in what it records. And of this I am proud in the diary; I did record essential things." Once again, there is tribute paid to the French novelist, Marcel Proust: "My self is like the self of Proust. It is an instrument to connect life and the myth."[20]

Always the pragmatist as she dreams, Nin makes her dreams useful. Perception does not merely tell us something; it does more; it connects diverse aspects of experience, one to another. Perception enables us to discern order in the chaos of experience. And in the modern age in which there is so much to know, to feel, to experience (partly because of the technology of recording and transmitting experience electronically), the self must be vast if man is to maintain psychic balance. Decades ago the Austrian writer Hermann Broch stated that "The only thing that can possibly match the enormous volume of our time is the volume of the I or the Self; and it, in turn, is so large that it cannot be expressed purely in novelistic form, but requires purely lyrical forms." Nin herself has written a passage that is strikingly similar, though more detailed, than Broch's thought: "The artist is aware of his self. He is aware that it is more than *his* self, that it is at once his guinea pig for experiments, his potential tool, his instrument, his camera, his computer to be nourished, his medium. When Proust says 'I' it is far more than the 'I' of Proust. It is an 'I' which contains many men, and far beyond that, it is a *symbol* of man. In this lies his objectivity."[21]

Nin is fully aware that her Diary has become much more than a personal document that traces the growth of an individual woman. After having struggled to "relinquish" her "secret," Nin has acknowledged that the Diary "belonged to everybody, and not only to me." Not everybody will wish to lay claim to Nin's Diary, and this is partly because Nin speaks with the voice of a woman, speaking not only for women and, beyond this, for the "sensitive Americans" to whom she dedicated *The Novel of the Future*. It is extraordinary but true that the first autobiography of the artist in the United States has been written by a woman. The always generous friend, James Leo Herlihy, perceived this extraordinary fact long ago in 1960 when he wrote to Nin:

> Through you, I have learned much about the workings of the artist, the artist in others and in myself, the process of the artist, his spirit and psychology, his endless discontent and the creation it fosters. This is the province of your work and the scope of your influence; it is your specialty, as they say, and you are magnificently qualified for it; no one else touches this material with even comparable incisiveness, power, beauty. I am talking about the material of your work, which is the artist himself, not his product. Your greatest body of work, your major achievement, is the journal itself, in which you have made palpable the very spirit of the artist; and as far as I know, no one in history has produced the equal of it.[22]

The Narcissus Pool

> The lake and the pond . . . are privileged with presence.
> Little by little, the dreamer is in this presence. . . . The soul
> is at home everywhere in a universe which reposes on the
> pond. The still water integrates all things, the universe and
> its dreamer.
>
> —Gaston Bachelard, *The Poetics of Reverie*

In one of her public talks Anaïs Nin tells her audience that the critic Leon Edel, in reviewing one of the Diaries, said that it was " 'nothing but a narcissus pool.' " Nin's reply was: ' "I have never seen a narcissus pool in which a thousand characters appeared at the same time.' "[1] One of the most valuable and perhaps the most original creations of the Diary is the writer Anaïs who, always evolving, writes of herself in a way that invites us to re-examine superficial attitudes toward the myth of Narcissus in favor of the deeper interpretation offered us, inadvertently, by the living portrait of the artist that the Diaries give their readers.

There are several versions of the story of Narcissus, but the most widely known is the account of Ovid in the third canto of the *Metamorphoses*. Narcissus was a beautiful boy of sixteen. He had rejected many aspiring lovers of both sexes, including the nymph Echo, whose passion and tragic fate were brought about by the jealous goddess Hera who suspected Echo of being Zeus' paramour. One of Narcissus' suffering lovers appealed to the goddess Nemesis to punish the lovely youth by making him fall hopelessly in love with an unattainable person. This Nemesis did. Beside a "lucid spring, gleaming like silver,"

158

. . . . the boy, tired with hunting and heat,
Stretched out to rest, charmed by the lovely spring.
He strove to quench his thirst, but other thirst
Was born—he was bewitched by his own beauty:
Loving a bodiless dream, and a body's shadow.
He saw himself with wonder, motionless
Poised, like a statue carved of Parian stone . . .
Now he desired himself, and loved his lover,
And sued his suitor, kindling his own flames.

When he could no longer endure the impossibility of embracing his beloved, Narcissus died of grief. His body disappeared and in its place was the yellow and white flower that we call the Narcissus, the "death flower" from the Greek word *narkao* ("stiff" or "dead"). In his essay "The Double as Immortal Self," Otto Rank records the version of this myth as related by Pausanius. Narcissus became inconsolable after the death of his twin sister, but when he discovered the reflection of his own image in the water, he was comforted, taking solace in the perfect resemblance of himself to the beloved sister.[2]

In his book *Myths of the Greeks and Romans,* Michael Grant says that Havelock Ellis was the first to use the term "narcissism" to describe pathological self-love, self-adoration so extreme that the love-struck victim is "dead" to the people and the events around him. A more narrow definition accuses the narcissist of onanism, of attempting to obtain sexual gratification from his own body. In common parlance narcissism is usually attributed to men who are thought to be effeminate or suspected to be homosexual and, of course, to women, who as a group are accused of being more vain than are men about their physical appearance. At its broadest, narcissism is regarded as simple selfishness.

From classical times to the modern age the figure of the lovely boy hopelessly in love with the reflection of his own image has attracted creative minds. It appears in the fourteenth century *Ovide Moralisé* and in the earlier thirteenth century *Roman de la Rose,* which was translated into English by Chaucer. Carvaggio treated the theme sympathetically. Poussin portrayed Narcissus in four different works to show the variety of feeling the subject can evoke. Milton borrowed Ovid's tale for his description of Eve. Two of the most important modern writers in France have treated the theme of Narcissus: André Gide in his second book, a Platonic study titled *Traité de Narcisse,* 1891, and Paul Valéry in two works, *Fragments du Narcisse,* published in *Charmes* of 1922, and *Cantate du Narcisse* for the composer Germaine Taillefer, in 1938. Rilke, who translated Valéry's *Fragments* into German, wrote two poems interpreting the tale of Narcissus in relation to the imagery of mirrors, a natural association because of the prominence of the still pond in the myth itself. Although Michael Grant does not analyze the significance of the Narcissus story specifically for the artist, he alludes to the particular relationship that Rank has written of in "The Double as Immortal Self," "Creative Urge and Personality," and "Life and Creation" from *Art and Artist;* and in other essays in which he describes the personality formation of the creative person. Discussing Rilke's "obsession" with Narcissus, Grant comments: "Through mirrors the artist, like many a gazer in folktales, projects himself into another dimension, overcoming his personal inhibitions and creating his own ideal, opposed though it may be to socially acceptable standards."[3]

Rank is the psychoanalyst who has devoted the greatest energy to the study of the creative personality type, and his insights into the artist are revealing and deep. His essential ideas are: that the first creative work produced by any artist is his own personality, brought to its particular nature through a sustained act of creative will; that the "average" or the "normal" type of personality seeks its immortality through procreation, through biological offspring; but that the artist, after a struggle, substitutes for collective immortality the individualized immortality of "deliberate self-expression in created works"; that in maturity the artist reproduces again and again in his work the unique self that he has laboriously developed through the course of his earlier life. The personal evolution of the artist moves through several stages, beginning with what Rank calls "self-nomination," and concluding with the affirmation of an expanded sense of self that finds its articulation in works of art. Rank contends that "the work of art is but the outward symbol of a profound psychological process within the artist whereby he manages finally to come to terms with an inborn human need to find something other and larger, outside the boundaries of the self, which he can then turn to account as the basis for living his life in the world." In his essay "Valéry's Dream of Narcissus," Wallace Fowlie inadvertently affirms Rank's view of the work of art as inevitably being a more or less complex self-portrait. "What began for Valéry as an exercise of meditation and contemplation was ultimately converted into a literary work, and notably into such a poem as *Fragments du Narcisse*. As the method of contemplation developed and matured, so did the desire to recast what was seen. Such a desire, for a poet, is his 'poetics,' his method of giving reality to the creatures and the creations of his mind . . . The composition of the poem . . . is the bringing to life of a secretive vision of the self. . . ."[4]

"Mais moi," asserts Valéry's Narcisse, "Narcisse aimé, je ne suis curieux/Que de ma seule essence."[5] Certainly, a conclusion of sterility is inevitable if the youth remains languishing beside the pool in a state of helpless passivity. Such a state implies consciousness severed from action, suffering, and eventually death at one's own hand, the suicide of Narcissus. This condition seems identical with neurosis. Writing of "Creation and Guilt" in *Truth and Reality,* Rank describes three personality types, the productive, the neurotic, and the average; and draws distinctions among them based on attitudes toward immortality and the responses evoked by seemingly inescapable guilt. The "average" type does not suffer from guilt because he conforms to the expectations of society, fulfills its obligations, receives its rewards, and attains immortality through the perpetuation of his biological image in children. The neurotic and the productive types are alike in being "different" from the average, in their rejection of social norms, and in their rebellion against procreation or the power of the biological force over life. The guilt that the neurotic experiences is paralyzing and, as a consequence, he is unable to create. The desire is thwarted by guilt; the more that time passes without production occurring, the more the neurotic is frustrated, anxious, depressed, and self-condemning. In Rank's view, then, the neurotic is an *artiste manqué*. Eventually, Rank redefines the "creative" type as the "productive" personality. The process through which the artist passes under the direction of creative will provides a model for what may be termed in a much more general sense the "productive" person. Such a person will have to pass through a process similar to that of the artist on his journey toward what Jung termed "self-individuation" or "self-realization."

In Rank's view narcissism represents a phase in the growth of a productive person. When Narcissus sees himself reflected in the pool, admires the image he contemplates and quite naturally loves this image, he is engaged in the search for himself. Michael Grant tells us that an Egyptian painting of Narcissus, contemporary with the *Metamorphoses,* identifies the figure of the youth as "Search" (*Zetema*). Stating his view of the original meaning of the tale of Narcissus, Edward F. Edinger in *Ego and Archetype* articulates an opinion that is similar to that of Rank without stressing the relationship between self-contemplation and the actual production of creative work. According to Edinger, "Narcissism in its original mythological implications is thus not a needless excess of self-love but rather just the opposite, a frustrated state of yearning for a self-possession which does not yet exist. The solution of the problem of Narcissus is the fulfillment of self-love rather than its renunciation . . . . Fulfilled self-love is a prerequisite to the genuine love of any object, and to the flow of psychic energy in general. In the case of Narcissus, fulfillment of self-love, or union with the image in the depths, requires a descent into the unconscious, a *nekyia,* or symbolic death. That this is the deeper meaning of the Narcissus myth is indicated by certain other details. After Narcissus died he turned into the flower narcissus. . . . The narcissus was sacred to Hades and opened the doors to his realm of the underworld. Persephone had just picked a narcissus when the earth opened up and Hades emerged to abduct her. The inescapable conclusion is that narcissism, at least in its original mythological sense, is the way into the unconscious where one must go in quest of individuality."[6]

A crucial transition must be made, however, before narcissism can lead to the necessary descent into the unconscious that precedes the second birth or the emergence into individuality. Narcissus must either lose consciousness of himself, specifically of his ego, before experiencing the symbolic death which the myth dramatizes as a prelude to the discovery of the self that is unique in each individual; or he must, in Rank's view, transform the meditative state into the productive state, as Fowlie observed of Valéry's process of writing *Fragments du Narcisse*. When Rank writes of the individual artist he always creates a counterpointed theme focusing on the stages of cultural growth as they are represented by specific works of art. Consequently, the judgment placed upon the Narcissus story reveals the orientation of a society toward the problem of immortalization. Of the Narcissus myth Rank writes, in the complicated context of "The Double as Immortal Self": "This lyrical tradition of decadent Greece, in which some modern psychologists claim to have found a symbolization of their self-love principle, appears to me as an anti-climax to the self-creative hero and his human representative, the artist-type. The latter's emergence was only possible by the renunciation of the egotistic principle of self-perpetuation in one's own image [procreation] and the substitution for it of the perpetuation of the self in work reflecting one's personality [creation]. In this sense, the sad story of the beautiful youth's early death seems to convey a warning to the individual not to cling to the easy belief in an immortal double by indulging in mere self-admiration. For even in the epoch of Greek tradition, a new religion of immortality had come into being, the deification of the hero, who, being himself mortal, successfully competed with the Gods. This idea of a self-creative power attributed to certain individuals signified a decisive step beyond the naive belief in an automatic survival of one's own double, in that it impressed upon man the conviction that he has to work for his immortality by creating lasting achievements. In this sense, the great Alberti, in the early fifteenth century, could say that when Narcissus saw his reflection in the water and trembled at the beauty of his own face he was the real inventor of painting."[7]

The origin of art is self-discovery. Self-discovery inspires self-love. Love of self establishes the source of power that engenders love of others and love of creative activity. A total commitment to self-discovery is a lifelong adventure that may bring to the explorer an amazing number and variety of masks for the self in its ceaseless motion away from the ego toward a collective identity. Wallace Fowlie recognizes this process in Valéry's absorption in the Narcissus myth: "Valéry uses the hero Narcissus as the adolescent in love with himself, but especially as the man engaged in self-analysis, who comes to realize the inexhaustibility, the endlessness of the self. . . ."[8]

Anaïs Nin's life work, the immense collage of experience, art, exploration, and dream, gives us both the books that exonerate the artist from the charge of selfishness and the history of a life devoted to the actualization of all its capabilities, not the least of which is the gift of love for others. A definite progress can be traced from the first published Diary to the sixth. The Anaïs of Diary I does exhibit narcissistic traits, but they did not circumscribe her feelings to her own person. She was generous toward others, interested in them, and clearly capable of loving them. Her struggle was to forge a belief in herself as a heroine, for without this she knew, as Rank knew, that she would be unable to fulfill her ideal of herself as an artist. When this part of the process had been completed, during the 1940s, Nin was strong enough to proceed to write the books she dreamed of creating. The surprise was that she did not have to limit herself to a few friends, to a few relationships, to a shrinking world. Her sense of self continued to deepen and to expand until, in the 1960s she had attained a depth of feminine sensibility that made Nin, without her wishing for the role, a leader of the women's movement. In her books and in her public talks she has articulated the feelings of hundreds of thousands of women. With feminine sensibility firmly integrated as part of this self, Nin's consciousness further expanded to include the awareness and aspirations of the creative person, male or female. The life so astonishingly revealed to us in the Diaries is a magnificent example in action of the creative will of which Rank wrote so much and in which he believed so fervently. Never, even when Nin was most intensely preoccupied with her unhappiness, was she unable to love other people. ". . . I had to

suffer from the concept that all diaries are narcissistic, that introspection is neurotic, when I knew that I overflowed with love of
others and that introspection was the only way to accomplish the
inner journey of self-creation."⁹

To "overflow" with love of others is one of Nin's achievements.
Her early work is a condemnation of self-love and of the incestuous
loves that often torment neurotics. In *House of Incest, Under a
Glass Bell,* "Stella," "Winter of Artifice" and "The Voice," Nin
exposes the crippling effects of fixation on the ego. Now that the
symbol of Narcissus has been reinterpreted, it is appropriate to
envision the body of Nin's work as a large pool in which there are
reflected at least a thousand faces and many many thousands more,
the faces of all those people who have found essential aspects of
themselves mirrored in her books. Consequently, Nin's work possesses a double significance: as works of art and as the record of
the lifelong evolution of a modern artist.

Water is the dominant and essential image of Nin's writing. Born
under the sign of Pisces, she constantly uses metaphors related to
water. One of the most memorable is Nin's clarification of the
nature of woman as "the mermaid with her fish-tail dipped in the
unconscious." A water image is the controlling figure in the passage in which she describes her one-time terror of losing the outlines
of herself in her identifications with others. The concept of flowing
and Nin's love of boats and ships as figures of speech have been
discussed in earlier chapters. One of her dreams is to own a house
by the edge of the sea. Conrad Moricand gave her a particularly
appropriate compliment when he said, "The fountain is the diary."
Among the metaphors Nin has used to describe the self is one that
reflects, once again, her affinity for water. In a letter to James Leo
Herlihy she wrote: "For me the self was merely an oceanic con-
tainer which could receive all experience. I never felt that this self
effaced others but served to relate to them."¹⁰

Water has always been associated with the process of creation in
art and life alike. Water is the source of all liquid matter. Traditionally, it represents the realm of the psyche. It is generally regarded as feminine. Water is the natural element of the artist. J. E.

Cirlot writes that "the concept of 'water' stands, of course, for all liquid matter. Moreover, the primaeval waters, the image of prime matter, also contained all solid bodies before they acquired form and rigidity. For this reason, the alchemists gave the name of 'water' to quicksilver in its first stage of transmutation and, by analogy, also to the 'fluid body' of man. This 'fluid body' is interpreted by modern psychology as a symbol of the unconscious, that is, of the non-formal, dynamic, motivating, female side of the personality. The projection of the mother-*imago* into the waters endows them with various numinous properties characteristic of the mother." In a statement that inadvertently affirms the significance of water in Nin's writing, Cirlot concludes, "Whether we take water as a symbol of the collective or of the personal unconscious, or else as an element of meditation and dissolution, it is obvious that this symbolism is an expression of the vital potential of the psyche, of the struggles of the psychic depths to find a way of formulating a clear message comprehensible to the consciousness."[11]

To create water is to create the source of life. Varda, the artist who was Nin's hero for many years, believed that what the artist aspires to do essentially is to recreate water. But even if he does not aspire to this superhuman goal, the artist must break through his fear of drowning and dive into the pool in search of the reality behind the image reflected on the still surface. The surface can be penetrated by the mind, as in Valéry's *Fragments du Narcisse,* or by intuition, as in the writing of Nin. Nin has expressed her amusement at Dali's appearing at a lecture in a diver's suit. She explained that ". . . water is the origin of birth and water has always symbolized the unconscious. The artist must always find his roots in that." It is important to remember the paradoxical nature of the image of Narcissus. The image can be penetrated without being dissolved. The impact of penetration may change the image, but it will not destroy it. As Gerard Genette writes in his essay "Complexe de Narcisse," the reflection in the pool is subject to "la fuite verticale," "la fuite en profondeur."[12]

Nin has always been confident that her own flight into depth would lead her to the intimacy she has dreamed of experiencing with the world. She has wanted her writing to draw her intensely into the world. And it has done so in a way that places beyond doubt the meaning of the narcissus pool in the life of this creative woman. At the end of one of her public talks she was asked: "Are you still writing in the diaries?"

Nin's answer was: "No, and it's your fault. I'm answering letters. But I think that that may be the natural outcome of a diary. . . . Perhaps that's the ultimate *raison d' etre* of the diary: that it ceases to be a solitary occupation and becomes a universal work. Perhaps that's the way it should end.

"I have talked about the continuity of the diary even though it takes different forms. At twenty it's different from thirty and at thirty it's different from at forty. And now it has changed again; this year it has become a correspondence with the world, and probably that is the right ending for a diary, that it would start as a river and then flow into an ocean and become an exchange of our more secret and private lives. . . . So I'm not worried about the metamorphosis of the diary which has now become universal, in other words, which has become *our* diary."[13]

Notes

Chapter 1   The Art of Ragpicking

1. *Novel,* p. 40. Nin uses "alchemy" repeatedly to describe the power of art.

2. Because Rimbaud's poetic doctrines and his attitudes toward dream and language have influenced Nin's writing, it is revealing to recall his prose poem "Alchimie du verbe." Nin continues Rimbaud's effort "to invent a poetic language accessible, one day or another, to all of the senses." This is why, as we shall see in the chapter on "symphonic writing," Nin has borrowed as many techniques as possible from painting, dance, and music. Wallace Fowlie, who has written extensively on French poetry and poets, has said of Rimbaud's poetic doctrine that it "seems to be a belief in the relationship which necessarily exists between a poem and witchcraft or magic or *sortilège,* as the French call it. A poem comes into being due to a process which, like alchemy, is magical and therefore foreign to the rules of logic and even the rules of instinct. According to this precept, a poem originates in this hidden life of the spirit and therefore is a reflection of this previous or submerged life." "Rimbaud: The Doctrine," *Age of Surrealism* (Bloomington: Indiana University Press, 1966 1st printing, 1950), p. 46.

3. In *The Novel of the Future,* Nin explains "The process of creativity is this daring escape from conventional patterns, not because they are conventional but because they are dead, used up," p. 128.

4. *Diary IV,* p. 219, 217, 219.

5. *Collages,* pp. 70–71.

6. *Beyond Painting,* "What Is Collage?", an excerpt reprinted in *Surrealists on Art,* ed. Lucy R. Lippard (Englewood Cliffs, N.J.: Prentice-Hall, 1970), 126.

7. *Selected Writings of Guillaume Apollinaire,* ed. and tr. Roger Shattuck (New York: New Directions, 1948), p. 233. In 1918 Apollinaire had already written *The Cubist Painters (Les Peintres cubistes* of 1912), and he had observed the ingenious use made by Picasso and Braque of *papiers collés,* dating from 1912 when Picasso inserted a piece of oilcloth into a painting. The Cubists were to invent a variety of ways of varying the relationships of planes and surfaces by combining painted and pasted elements. Collage, however, has a history that stretches beyond modern art into twelfth-century Japan and to Persia of the thirteenth century. Collage includes the iconography of Russia and certain popular art forms like posters, ash trays, and paperweights *(kitsch)* made in the late nineteenth century in Europe. Before the twentieth century, however, collage forms were primarily decorative. Herta Wescher, author of a detailed study of collage, writes: "Not until the twentieth cen-

tury, when creative artists took to working with it, did collage become a new and valid means of expression, one which has left its mark indelibly on the art of today," *Collage,* tr. Robert E. Wolf (New York: Harry N. Abrams, 1968), p. 19.

8. Louis Aragon, from *Challenge to Painting,* an excerpt reprinted in *Surrealists on Art,* p. 38; Ernst, p. 131.

9. There are many ways of fusing the elements of a collage besides pasting: for example; nailing; tying; sewing; welding; printing. In literature collage is created by juxtaposition. It may, as in the case of Apollinaire's own *Calligrammes of* 1918, involve the implementation of the spatial properties of the page with the words; or it may more simply depend upon combinations of types of writing which do not contain the traditional connectives (patterns of time, space, characters, incidents, themes, even transitions). In both methods the result will be that sense of novelty or surprise which Apollinaire and the Surrealists prized so highly as an effect of the "new" art.

10. In "The Art of Stillness," the essay which concludes his book *The Banquet Years,* Roger Shattuck distinguishes between heterogeneous and homogeneous modes of juxtaposition. Surrealist writing displays the former, and quite deliberately so, since it depends for its power of transformation upon violent contrast; so, too, does montage composition in film when it follows the ideal of its inventor, Serge Eisenstein. When the elements juxtaposed are more nearly homogeneous, however, the composition will give a calmer, a more serene impression, perhaps a sense of an underlying, if subtly patterned, unity.

11. *Novel,* p. 33.

12. *Novel,* p. 128.

13. "Life and Creation," *Art and Artist,* tr. from the German by Charles Francis Atkinson (New York: Agathon Press, 1968), pp. 47-48, 49-50.

14. "The Voice," *Winter,* p. 123.

15. *Diary II,* p. 106. Echoing Nin's ambitious project is Rosalyn Drexler's statement about a cross she sculpted from wood and rusty metal: "It was bought from my first show in 1960 and at the time, I couldn't believe that anyone else would want to own it. But I can understand it hanging in a church with all the gold and glitter and precious stained-glass windows. What has been discarded, used, thrown away is still holy—if not holier. I think art and religion are very close—the spirit of reclamation and love." "Dialogue," by Elaine de Kooning with Rosalyn Drexler, *Art and Sexual Politics,* eds. Thomas B. Hess and Elizabeth C. Baker (New York: Macmillan, 1973), p. 69.

16. "Ragtime," *Bell,* p. 58.

17. *Ibid.*

18. "Ragtime," *Bell,* p. 59, 61.

19. "Ragtime," *Bell,* p. 62.

20. *Collages,* p. 69.

21. *Collages,* p. 91.

22. *Memories, Dreams, Reflections,* ed. Aniela Jaffe; tr. from the German by Richard and Clara Winston (New York: Random House, 1961), p. 397.

23. *The Writer and the Symbols,* p. 37.

24. *Novel,* pp. 84-85, 36.

25. Nin does not seem to distinguish between *fuse* and *merge.* In English, as in French, to fuse means "to unite or blend." But "to merge" is different because the joined parts do not remain equal; in a merger, one partner is *submerged* in the other. For a metaphysical approach to fusion, see Gaston Bachelard, *The Poetics of Reverie: Childhood, Language, and the Cosmos,* tr. from the French by Daniel Russell (Boston: Beacon Press, 1969: 1st French edition, 1960) pp. 197-98.

26. *Diary IV,* p. 154.

27. *Novel,* p. 68.

28. *Lawrence,* p. 20.

29. *Winter,* pp. 90-91.

30. *Surrealists on Art,* p. 127.

31. *Diary II,* p. 321.

32. *Diary IV,* p. 157.

33. *Diary VI,* p. 280.

34. *Novel,* p. 33.

Chapter 2   Symphonic Writing

1. *Diary I,* pp. 56-57.

2. *The Writer and the Symbols,* p. 35.

3. See "Proceed from the Dream," *A Woman Speaks,* p. 118.

4. See Rimbaud's famous letters, "Les Lettres du Voyant," which are often printed in volumes of his poetry. Also see "A New Center of Gravity" and "The Artist as Magician" in *A Woman Speaks. In Favor of the Sensitive Man and Other Essays* contains a section on "Writing, Music, and Films."

5. "The Artist as Magician," *A Woman Speaks,* p. 188. Nin must often defend herself against attacks for making artists her subjects. For the sort of attack that is typical, see the question on p. 195 of *A Woman Speaks.* In the literature of the U.S., Nin's interest in and defense of the artist is virtually unprecedented.

6. The atttempt to restore spiritual meaning to life is, of course, typical of Romanticism and of neo-Romantic movements. This attempt follows industrialization. In England it begins with Blake; in Italy, the themes of the English Romantic poets appear as recently as the decades following World War II. The most influential and perhaps the most metaphysical of the modern statements in defense of spirit is Wassily Kandinsky's *Concern-*

ing the Spiritual in Art, first published in 1912. The struggle against empiricism also unites the Symbolists and the Surrealists.

7. *Anaïs Nin Reader,* ed. Philip K. Jason (Chicago: The Swallow Press, 1973), pp. 28-29.

8. *Diary V,* p. 91, 92.

9. "Proceed from the Dream," *A Woman Speaks,* p. 129.

10. *Diary IV,* p. 150.

11. *Diary V,* pp. 92-93.

12. See "The Artist as Magician," *A Woman Speaks,* pp. 188-89, for Nin's remarks about poetic language. Everything in *The Novel of the Future* is related to this point; the book makes an excellent resource for creative writing courses.

13. See "The Artist as Magician," *A Woman Speaks,* p. 213. Here and throughout the Diary Nin protests against the Surrealist practice of automatic writing.

14. "The Eye's Journey," *Bell,* p. 78.

15. "Through the Streets of My Own Labyrinth," *Bell,* p. 69.

16. "The Eye's Journey," *Bell,* p. 78.

17. See "Proceed from the Dream," *A Woman Speaks,* p. 118: "An artist like Varda could have taught us how to live. At fifteen if I had met Varda I would have learned how to live from him."

18. *Winter,* p. 88.

19. *Winter,* pp. 84-85, 88.

20. *Winter,* p. 99.

21. *Winter,* p. 113, 100.

22. "Stella," *Winter,* p. 27; "The Voice," *Winter,* p. 161, 126.

23. *Cities,* "Spy," pp. 429-30.

24. *Diary II,* p. 6. In "Children", the shoemaker with whom Djuna shares a love of beautiful shoes, has a club foot.

25. *Cities,* "Seduction," p. 521.

26. *Cities,* "Children," pp. 130-31, 132, 167, 165-67, 150-51, 197.

27. *House,* p. 72. J. E. Cirlot in *A Dictionary of Symbols,* tr. from the Spanish by Jack Sage (New York: Philosophical Library, 1962), pp. 72-73, writes of dance: "The corporeal image of a given process, or of becoming, or of the passage of time. In Hindu doctrine, the dance of Shiva in his role as Nataraja (The King of the Cosmic Dance, symbolizing the union of space and time within evolution) clearly has this meaning. There is a universal belief that, in so far as it is a rhythmic art-form, it is a symbol of the act of creation. This is why the dance is one of the most ancient forms of magic."

28. For references to Martha Graham, see *Diary IV,* p. 120, 131. See also *Diary V,* p. 88, 246, and *A Woman Speaks,* p. 112.

29. *Diary IV,* pp. 130-31.

30. "Stella," *Winter,* p. 28. See *Diary VI,* pp. 37-38, for references to Klee. Some of the other artists mentioned in Diary VI, which is much concerned with the cultural life of New York and California, are Varda, of course; Jean Tinguely, Richard Lippold, Alexander Calder, and Ian Hugo.

31. *Cities,* "Spy," p. 450.

32. *Cities,* "Spy," p. 452.

33. *Cities,* "Ladders," p. 95, 83.

34. *Cities,* "Seduction," p. 507.

35. See Cirlot, the entry on alchemy, pp. 6-8. In "Refusal to Despair," *A Woman Speaks,* pp. 19-20, Nin talks of the difference between her views of transparency and transcending.

36. *Cities,* "Ladder," p. 89, 90, 116; "Heart," pp. 241, 250, 253, 265, 267.

37. This analysis of the structure of *Cities of the Interior* has been printed: "Anais Nin's 'Continuous Novel' *Cities of the Interior,*" *A Casebook on Anais Nin,* ed. Robert Zaller (New York: New American Library, 1974), pp. 65-76.

38. Walter H. Sokel, *The Writer in Extremis: Expressionism in Twentieth Century German Literature* (Stanford, California: Stanford University Press, 1959), p. 26 In *Diary VI* Nin refers to the influence of her "inner music" on *Solar Barque.* Among the composers whose work she discusses in this volume are Satie; Louis and Bebe Barron; Peggy Glanville-Hicks; and the contemporary style called *musique concrète.*

39. For references to jazz, see *Novel,* pp. 28-29, 82, 89-91; *Diary III,* p. 36; and *Diaries V* and *VI.* In "Ladders" *(Cities,* p. 478), jazz is called the "music of the body."

40. *Diary II,* p. 53.

41. *Diary IV,* p. 40.

42. *Diary II,* p. 314.

43. 'Stella," *Winter,* p. 8, 25, 26. Lillian attempts to "seek in music that wholeness which she could not find in love . . ." *Cities,* p. 210. This does not work for her, any more than for Rango's aunt, a musician who, unhappy in marriage, gradually starves to death after staying up night after night playing the music of Bach and Beethoven.

44. *Cities,* "Spy," p. 462.

45. *Cities,* "Spy," p. 382.

46. *Cities,* "Spy," p. 391.

47. *Cities,* "Spy," p. 432.

48. Schopenhauer wrote: "The unutterable depth of all music by virtue of which it floats through our consciousness as the vision of a paradise firmly believed in yet ever distant from us, and by which also it is so fully understood and yet so inapplicable, rests on the fact that it restores to us all the emotions of our inmost nature, but entirely without reality and far removed

from their pain," *The World as Will and Idea,* tr. by R. B. Haldane and J. Kemp (Garden City: New York: Doubleday and Co., 1961), p. 275.

49. *Winter,* p. 100.

50. *Cities,* "Heart," p. 268; "Seduction," p. 493; "Children," pp. 237-38. For Nin's remarks on music and continuity, see *A Woman Speaks,* pp. 182-83.

51. *Cities,* "Spy," pp. 461-62.

Chapter 3   The Dream

1. *Cities,* "Heart," p. 288.

2. "Furrawn," *A Woman Speaks,* p. 259.

3. "Refusal to Despair," *A Woman Speaks,* p. 21.

4. *Diary II,* p. 152.

5. *Diary IV,* p. 120.

6. *The Writer and the Symbols,* p. 39.

7. *Memories, Dreams, Reflections,* ed. Aniela Jaffe; tr. from the German by Richard and Clara Winston (New York: Random House, 1961), p. 401.

8. *Novel,* p. 5. See Gaston Bachelard, *The Poetics of Reverie.*

9. C. G. Jung, "Dreams," *Psychological Reflections,* ed. Jolande Jacobi (New York: Harper & Row, 1961), p. 67.

10. *Diary III,* p. 300.

11. *The Writer and the Symbols,* p. 39.

12. *Diary IV,* p. 127.

13. Jung wrote: "One could say, with a little exaggeration, that the persona is that which in reality one is not, but which oneself as well as others think one is." The task of life, according to Jung, is to discover the authentic self and to live the life that best expresses it. See *Memories, Dreams, Reflections,* p. 397. (It seems clear that Nin agrees with this point of view.)

14. See "Abstraction," *The Novel of the Future.*

15. *Cities,* "Ladder," p. 5.

16. *Diary IV,* p. 139.

17. *Diary V,* p. 93, 91.

18. Originally, Stella was to have been included in *Cities,* but she was dropped because of her failure to develop into a mature woman.

19. *Diary IV,* p. 41, 81.

20. *Diary V,* p. 123.

21. *The Poetics of Reverie: Childhood, Language, and the Cosmos,* tr. from the French by David Russell (Boston: Beacon Press, 1971), p. 59. See especially "Animus—Anima." Bachelard's books on the philosophy of imagery will interest readers of Nin. See *The Poetics of Space* and *The Psychoanalysis of Fire.*

22. *House,* p. 62.

23. "The Voice," *Winter*, p. 169. See also *Diary IV*, p. 124, for an expression of the conflict dreams present by drawing one away from outer reality: "The dreamlike quality of experience both cheats one of reality and yet creates a world of wonder."

24. Djuna Barnes, *Nightwood* (New York: Harcourt Brace, 1937; New Directions, 1961), p. 81, 83-84.

25. "Proceed from the Dream," *A Woman Speaks*, p. 120.

26. *Diary II*, p. 281, 11.

27. Nin admires the books of Antoine de Saint-Exupéry, the French author and aviator.

28. *Cities*, "Spy," p. 390, 389.

29. *Novel*, pp. 20-21; *Diary III*, p. 30. More passages on boats can be found in *A Woman Speaks*, pp. 122-24, and in *Diary II*, pp. 112-113. See *Diary V* for descriptions of the solar barque that plays such an important role in *Seduction of the Minotaur*.

30. *Winter*, p. 157, 159.

31. *Winter*, p. 169.

32. *Winter*, p. 120.

33. *Winter*, p. 124, 145.

34. *Winter*, p. 137, 140.

35. *Diary III*, p. 300, 301. See also "Refusal to Despair" and "The Personal Life Deeply Lived" in *A Woman Speaks*.

36. *Cities*, "Seduction," p. 487, 565.

37. *Cities*, "Seduction," p. 560, 505, 529.

38. *Cities*, "Seduction," p. 486.

39. *Cities*, "Seduction," p. 565, 567.

40. *Cities*, "Seduction," pp. 588-89.

41. See, for example, the Magic Theatre section that brings Hesse's *Steppenwolf* to its conclusion. In Diary IV, pp. 70-71, Nin speaks of how analysis bombards the psyche just as the atom is split to release energy.

42. "The Voice," *Winter*, p. 170, 175. Julio Cortázar, who admires this passage, quotes it in *Hopscotch, Rayuela* (New York, New American Library, 1971), p. 470. This novel was first published in Spanish in 1963.

43. *Diary II*, p. 216.

44. *Diary II*, p. 152; also *Cities*, "Heart," p. 288; *Diary IV*, p. 62.

Chapter 4   Rediscovering Woman

1. *Diary I*, p. 223.

2. *Diary III*, p. 264.

3. *Diary I*, p. 165.

4. *Diary II*, p. 209.

5. "An Interview with Anais Nin," Sharon Spencer, *Shantih: Interna-*

tional Writings (Winter/Spring, 1972), p. 31.

6. *Diary I*, pp. 164-165, p. 71.

7. *Diary I*, pp. 340-348.

8. *Diary I*, p. 360.

9. *Winter*, p. 119.

10. *Diary I*, p. 346.

11. *Diary I*, p. 290.

12. *Diary I*, p. 354.

13. See *Diary V* for an analysis of the temporary return of this longing for a father in Nin's relationship with Max Pfeffer.

14. *Diary IV*, pp. 141-42.

15. *Cities*, "Ladders," p. 64, 124.

16. *Cities*, "Seduction," p. 543.

17. *Cities*, "Seduction," p. 479.

18. *Cities*, "Children," p. 173.

19. *Cities*, "Heart," p. 358.

20. *House*, p. 27, 21.

21. *House*, p. 48.

22. *House*, pp. 51-52, 55.

23. *House*, p. 62, 71.

24. *Cities*, "Ladder," p. 104.

25. *Cities*, "Heart," p. 344.

26. In the *Shantih* interview quoted earlier in this chapter, Nin states her belief that woman, like man, should be able to maintain multiple relationships without being condemned or punished.

27. *Cities*, "Spy," p. 450, 451.

28. *Cities*, "Spy," p. 452, 453.

29. *Diary II*, p. 109.

30. *Diary I*, p. 273.

31. *A Room of One's Own* (New York: Harcourt, Brace and World, 1929), p. 35.

32. *Diary V*, p. 223.

33. *Diary, I*, p. 69.

34. *Diary III*, p. 50, 53.

35. *Diary III*, p. 239.

36. *Woman's Mysteries Ancient and Modern* (New York: G. P. Putnam's Sons for the C. G. Jung Foundation, 1971; New York: Longmans Green, 1935), p. 111.

37. *Woman's Mysteries*, p. 105, 102, 103.

38. *Shantih*, pp. 30-31.

39. Nin's erotic writing will soon be published by Harcourt, Brace Jovanovich.

40. *Diary V*, p. 214.

41. "Eroticism in Women," *In Favor of the Sensitive Man and Other Essays* (New York: Harcourt Brace Jovanovich, 1976), p. 11.

Chapter 5   Transforming the Muse

1. See my article "Femininity and the Woman Writer: Doris Lessing's *The Golden Notebook* and the *Diary* of Anais Nin," *Woman's Studies* (Vol. 1, No. 3, 1973), pp. 247-57. See as well, Lawrence J. Hatterer, "The Woman Artist," *The Artist in Society* (New York: Grove Press, 1965), pp. 172-78. The Jungian analysts M. Esther Harding and Irene Claremont de Castillejo discuss the woman artist along with other women who develop strong work commitments outside the home. See their books, respectively *The Way of All Women* and *Knowing Woman*. Relevant, too, are essays by Cynthia Ozick, Elaine Showalter and Linda Nochlin in *Woman in Sexist Society,* ed. Vivian Gornick and Barbara K. Moran (New York: Basic Books, 1971), pp. 431-51.

2. "Hedja," *Bell,* p. 86.

3. M. Esther Harding, *Woman's Mysteries Ancient and Modern* (New York: Longmans Green, 1935; New York: G. P. Putnam's Sons for the C. G. Jung Foundation, 1971), p. 111.

4. Otto Rank, "Feminine Psychology and Masculine Ideology," *Beyond Psychology* (Philadelphia: E. Hauser, 1941; New York, Dover Publications, 1958), p. 250.

5. *Novel,* p. 39.

6. "Hedja," *Bell,* p. 87, 88, 90.

7. Ibid., p. 91.

8. Ibid, p. 92, 93.

9. Ibid, p. 95.

10. Harding, *The Way of All Women,* pp. 78-79.

11. Hatterer, pp. 173-74.

12. Otto Rank, "Life and Creation," *Art and Artist: Creative Urge and Personality Development,* tr. from the German by Charles Francis Atkinson (New York: Alfred A. Knopf, 1932; New York: Agathon Press, 1968), pp. 44-45.

13. Tillie Olsen, "Silences," *The Harvard Advocate* (CVI, No. 2/3; Winter, 1973), p. 79.

14. *Novel,* p. 144.

15. *Diary III,* p. 234. See *Diary I,* p. 81 and p. 163 for Nin's relationship with René Allendy.

16. *Diary II,* p. 117.

17. *Diary II,* p. 31.

18. *Diary I,* p. 309. For Nin's evaluation of Rank's role in helping her develop creative identity, see "Proceed from the Dream," *A Woman Speaks,* p. 40, 146.

19. *Diary II*, p. 24, 172, 110.

20. "Glossary," *Memories, Dreams, Reflections, ed.* by Aniela Jaffé, tr. from the German by Richard and Clara Winston (New York: Random House, 1961), p. 39.

21. *Diary III*, p. 239. On p. 260 of *Diary III* Nin comments on Jaeger's capacity to bring to her treatment the insights of a woman: "Jaeger, by being true to the woman, creating the woman in me, by her particular intuition as a woman, has penetrated truths not observed by either Allendy or Rank. The creator's guilt in me has to do with my femininity, my subjection to man."

22. *Diary IV*, p. 10.

23. *Diary III*, p. 259.

24. Rank, *Art and Artist*, p. 52.

25. Rank, *Art and Artist*, p. 61.

26. *Diary V*, p. 100.

27. C. G. Jung, "Anima and Animus," *Two Essays on Analytical Psychology* (New York: C. G. Jung Foundation), p. 220.

28. Emma Jung, *Animus and Anima: Two Essays* (New York: Analytical Psychology of New York, 1969), p. 13.

29. Emma Jung, p. 29.

30. *Diary III*, p. 100, 144.

31. *Diary III*, p. 260.

32. See *Diary II*, pp. 231-36. The specific quotations are from p. 234, 269, 235.

33. *Diary II*, pp. 235-36.

34. *Diary V*, p. 30.

35. *Diary IV*, p. 150.

36. *Diary IV*, p. 25.

37. "Stella," *Winter*, p. 10.

38. "Stella," *Winter*, p. 16, 54.

39. *Diary II*, p. 145.

40. *Diary V*, p. 131.

41. *Diary III*, p. 173.

Chapter 6   Anais: Her Book

1. *Diary III*, p. 165.

2. *Diary I*, p. 243.

3. "Approaching the Unconscious," *Man and His Symbols*, ed. Carl G. Jung (New York: Dell Publishing Co., 1968), pp. 1-94.

4. *Diary I*, p. 280.

5. Ibid.

6. *Diary II*, p. 172.

7. *Novel*, p. 155.

178   *Collage of Dreams*

8. *Diary II*, p. 167.
9. *Diary III*, p. 314.
10. See *Diary VI*, pp. 382-84. Two distinguished men of publishing, Alan Swallow and Hiram Haydn, were responsible for bringing out Nin's Diary.
11. *Diary II*, p. 110.
12. *Novel*, p. 85. The question of the extent to which Nin's published Diary has been edited and polished is not totally clear. The Diaries themselves contain many references to a process that suggests rewriting, cutting and polishing, but in "The Personal Life Deeply Lived," *A Woman Speaks*, pp. 148-49, Nin denies rewriting and explains what sort of material has been deleted from the published Diaries (see p. 175, 177, 179).

Still another (unconscious) form of editing is discussed by Karen Horney in *Self-Analysis* (New York: W. W. Norton and Co., Inc., 1942), pp. 188-89: "A diary often glances with one eye toward a future reader, whether that reader be the writer at a future time or a wider audience. Any such side glance at posterity, however, inevitably detracts from pristine honesty. Deliberately or inadvertently the writer is bound, then, to do some retouching. He will omit certain factors entirely, minimize his shortcomings or blame them on others, protect other people from exposure. The same will happen when he writes down his associations if he takes the least squint at an admiring audience or at the idea of creating a masterpiece of unique value. He will then commit all those sins that undermine the value of free associations. Whatever he sets down on paper should serve one purpose only, that of recognizing himself." Horney, of course, is not talking about the diary as art, the diary as written by an artist, but the diary as an aid in the process of a self-analysis. Nevertheless, her remarks are interesting enough to be included here.

13. *Diary I*, p. 359.
14. *Diary II*, p. 235.
15. *Diary III*, p. 176.
16. *Diary III*, p. 14.
17. *Diary III*, p. 53.
18. *Diary IV*, p. 143, 142.
19. *Diary IV*, p. 165, 126, 187.
20. *Diary IV*, p. 221.
21. *Diary IV*, p. 225.
22. *Diary V*, p. 106.
23. *Diary V*, p. 239. There are moments during the years of *Diary VI* when Nin still feels that Herlihy is her only appreciative reader. Their correspondence is one of the liveliest aspects of *Diary VI* and the most intellectually stimulating.
24. *Diary V*, p. 181.

25. *Diary V*, p. 166.

26. In earlier volumes it has been travel to foreign countries that has brought a sense of renewal and rebirth to Nin; in *Diary VI* it is primarily her several trips to France which represent a journeying homeward.

27. *Diary VI*, p. 360.

28. *Diary VI*, pp. 374-75.

29. A fine selection of Nin's reviews, interviews and travel pieces is *In Favor of the Sensitive Man and Other Essays* (New York: Harcourt Brace Jovanovich, 1976).

30. *Diary VI*, p. 332.

31. *Diary VI*, pp. 248-49.

32. See *Diary VI*, pp. 387-88.

33. *Diary VI*, p. 85, 30, 298, 216, 215, 146-47. The most perceptive insights into the Diary are those of James Leo Herlihy; see, for example, p. 45, 95-96, and 219. Also excellent is Robert Kirsch's *Los Angeles Times* review which is quoted on pp. 397-99.

34. *Diary VI*, pp. 277-78. Nin's surprising championship of the "objective" is interestingly stated as an analogy to Rimbaud's having given up poetry: "Like Rimbaud, I am walking out of my poetic world, so definitely unwanted. I am starting now as a diary writer and realist. For the rest of my life I will be at work on this. The poetry and the fairy tales (Oliver Evans called *Collages* The Arabian Nights) have isolated and alienated me too much," *Diary VI*, pp. 298-99.

35. *Diary VI*, p. 25, 379.

36. *Diary VI*, 378.

37. *Diary VI*, pp. 244-45.

Chapter 7   The "Journal des Autres"

1. In "The Personal Life Deeply Lived," *A Woman Speaks*, p. 161, Nin denies that the Diary is a *Recherche du temps perdu:* "I did not wish to recapture the past. It [the Diary] is actually a seeking to unite the past, the present, and the future." This distinction is important to an understanding of Nin's personal relationship to time, but it does not alter the fact that there are profound similarities between her novel-cycle and her Diary and Proust's group of interconnected novels.

The reference to the "gods of the deep" is to *Diary III*, p. 256.

2. See "The Artist as Magician," *A Woman Speaks*, p. 207, for an enumeration of the writers who have influenced Nin's work. A summary of Proust's meaning to her can be found in "Out of the Labyrinth," *In Favor of the Sensitive Man*, p. 75.

3. For remarks about Proust's approach to characterization, see *Diary*

III, p. 51; *Diary IV*, p. 28; *Diary V*, p. 123; *Novel*, pp. 62-63. The quotation is from *Diary V*, p. 255.

The passage about style can be found in *Diary III*, p. 133, and Nin' thoughts about Proust's treatment of the "half-dream" are in Diary II, p. 51 and *Novel*, p. 8, 121.

4. The organic, flowing, cellular structure of Proust's work is much dis cussed by Nin, and always praised. *Diary IV*, p. 17; *Diary VI*, p. 66, 321 386; *Diary V*, pp. 92-93; *Novel*, p. 42, 162.

5. *Diary I*, p. 290.

6. *Diary II*, p. 111; *Diary III*, p. 163; *Diary II*, p. 14; *Diary II*, p. 235 *Novel*, p. 196

7. *Diary II*, p. 167, 22, 250, 285, 285-86.

8. *Diary VI*, p. 354; *Diary II*, p. 103; *Diary VI*, p. 381.

9. *Diary V*, p. 112.

10. *Diary V*, p. 101; *Diary IV*, p. 127.

11. "The Voice," *Winter*, pp. 174-75.

12. *Diary IV*, p. 153. See also *Diary VI*, p. 248, for Nin's comparison of Proust's and Durrell's "geometry of space" and "psychology in space and time."

13. *Diary V*, p. 194; *Novel*, p. 61; *Diary VI*, p. 85.

14. The Rimbaud quotation is in the famous letter to Paul Demeny dated May 15, 1871. For more ideas on the complicated use of the mask in personality development, see W. B. Yeats' book *A Vision*. See "The Personal Life Deeply Lived," *A Woman Speaks*, pp. 167-68, for Nin's comments on how the woman is only complete when the diary is considered as part of her total self. The direct address to the Diary is from *Diary I*, p. 243.

15. *Diary II*, p. 285.

16. *Diary II*, p. 285; *Diary IV*, p. 129. Readers with an interest in psychology may want to look at my article "The Dream of Twinship in the Writings of Anaïs Nin," *Journal of the Otto Rank Association*, Vol. 9, No. 2, Winter, 1974-75.

17. *Diary II*, pp. 210-11, p. 222. In the third *Diary* and in *The Novel of the Future*, Nin corrects this early criticism of Proust.

18. "The Personal Life Deeply Lived," *A Woman Speaks*, p. 180. For Nin's decision to write the "Journal des autres," see *Diary VI*, pp. 319-20, and p. 328, which describes Marguerite Young's reaction to the idea.

19. *Diary II*, p. 109; *Diary I*, p. 273; *Novel*, p. 36.

20. "The Unveiling of Woman," *A Woman Speaks*, p. 107; "The Personal Life Deeply Lived," *A Woman Speaks*, p. 162; *Diary II*, p. 232.

21. Quoted by Theodore Ziolkowski, *Hermann Broch:* Columbia Essays on Modern Writers, No. 3 (New York: Columbia University Press, 1964), p. 19; *Novel*, p. 37.

22. "The Personal Life Deeply Lived," *A Woman Speaks,* p. 162; *Diary VI,* p. 219.

Chapter 8 The Narcissus Pool

1. "The Personal Life Deeply Lived," *A Woman Speaks,* pp. 155-56.
2. The passage from the *Metamorphoses* is quoted by Michael Grant, *Myths of the Greeks and Romans* (New York: New American Library, p. 334.) *Beyond Psychology* (New York: Dover Publications, Inc., 1958; first published by E. Hauser, Philadelphia, 1941), p. 98.
3. See Grant, pp. 333-37. The quotation is on p. 337. The association of mirrors with water and the capacity for reflection is ancient and complex. Rank, in "The Double as Immortal Self" and Edward F. Edinger, in *Ego and Archetype,* connect the story of the conception of Dionysios when his mother gazed into a mirror with the myth of Narcissus.
4. Rank's exceedingly complex theory of the artist, his development, his relation to myth, to history, and to the collective is found in *Art and Artist, Beyond Psychology,* and *Truth and Reality.* The quotation is from Vern Haddick, "Artist, Self and Art, a Review of *George Eliot: The Emergent Self,* by Ruby F. Redinger." *Journal of the Otto Rank Association* (Summer, 1976), p. 28. *Climate of Violence: The French Literary Tradition from Baudelaire to the Present* (London: Secker & Warburg, 1969), pp. 73-74.
5. Quoted by Fowlie, p. 83.
6. *Ego and Archetype: Individuation and the Religious Function of the Psyche* (New York: G. P. Putnam's Sons for the C. G. Jung Foundation for Analytical Psychology, pp. 161-62.
7. *Beyond Psychology,* pp. 98-99.
8. "Valery's Dream of Narcissus," *Climate of Violence,* p. 76.
9. "The Personal Life Deeply Lived," *A Woman Speaks,* pp. 155-56.
10. *Diary II,* p. 235; 315. Valéry and Gide often walked in the botanical garden at Montpelier where there was a tomb inscribed *Placandis Narcissae manibus* ("To appease the shades of Narcissa"). *Diary VI,* p. 45. In "The Artist as Magician," *A Woman Speaks,* Nin defends herself against the accusation of remoteness from life: ". . . critics . . . labeled me as very far away from life. I wasn't far away at all. I was like Cousteau, at a level like the bottom of the sea, where they couldn't follow," p. 200.
11. *A Dictionary of Symbols,* tr. from the Spanish by Jack Sage (New York: Philosophical Library, 1962), pp. 345-46.
12. "The Artist as Magician," *A Woman Speaks,* p. 201. Genette, *Figures I* (Paris: Seuil, 1966), pp. 23-24.
13. "The Personal Life Deeply Lived," *A Woman Speaks,* p. 179-180.

A Selected Bibliography

Bibliographical Note: The items included here are those actually consulted for the book. I have made no attempt to compile a bibliography of works by Anaïs Nin or of books and articles about her. This has been done admirably by Benjamin Franklin V of the University of Michigan: *Anaïs Nin: A Bibliography*, published by the Kent State University Press in 1973. Reesa Marcinczyk has recently completed "A Checklist of the Writings of Anaïs Nin, 1973-1976"; this checklist updates Franklin's bibliography and appears in *Under the Sign of Pisces: Anaïs Nin and Her Circle*, a newsletter published by the Ohio State University Libraries and edited by Richard R. Centing since its initial appearance in 1970. *Under the Sign of Pisces* is invaluable to any student of Nin's writings. Besides her books, Nin has published more than 150 articles, reviews, prefaces, and interviews.

    Collage of Dreams is the third book of criticism on Nin's writings to appear in English. The first is *Anaïs Nin* by Oliver Evans, 1968; the second is *The Mirror and the Garden: Realism and Reality in the Writings of Anaïs Nin* by Evelyn Hinz, 1971.

Apollinaire, Guillaume, *Selected Writings*. Translated from the French and edited by Roger Shattuck. New York: New Directions, 1948.

Bachelard, Gaston. *The Poetics of Reverie: Childhood, Language and the Cosmos*. Translated from the French by Daniel Russell. Boston: The Beacon Press, 1969 (first French edition, 1960).

————. *The Poetics of Space*. Translated from the French by Maria Jolas. Boston: The Beacon Press, 1969 (first French edition, 1958).

————. *The Psychoanalysis of Fire*. Translated from the French by

Alan C. M. Ross. Boston: The Beacon Press, 1964 (first French edition, 1938).

Barnes, Djuna, *Nightwood*. New York: New Directions, 1961 (Harcourt Brace, 1937).

Cirlot, J. E. *A Dictionary of Symbols*. Translated from the Spanish by Jack Sage. New York: The Philosophical Library, 1962.

Claremont, Irene De Castillejo. *Knowing Woman*. New York: G. P. Putnam's Sons for the C. G. Jung Foundation, 1973.

Cortázar, Julio. *Hopscotch*. Translated from the Spanish by Gregory Rabassa. New York: New American Library, 1971 (Spanish edition, 1963).

Edinger, Edward F. *Ego and Archetype: Individuation and the Religious Function of the Psyche*. New York: G. P. Putnam's Sons for the C. G. Jung Foundation, 1972.

Evans, Oliver. *Anaïs Nin*. Carbondale and Edwardsville, Illinois: Southern Illinois University Press, 1968.

Fowlie, Wallace. *Age of Surrealism*. Bloomington, Indiana: Indiana University Press, 1960 (published by arrangement with Alan Swallow).

———. *Climate of Violence: The French Literary Tradition from Baudelaire to the Present*. London: Secker and Warburg, 1969.

Franklin, Benjamin. *Anaïs Nin: A Bibliography*. The Serif Series: Number 29, Bibliographies and Checklists, William White, general editor. Kent, Ohio: The Kent State University Press, 1973.

Gornick, Vivian and Barbara K. Moran, eds. *Woman in Sexist Society*. New York: Basic Books, 1971.

Grant, Michael. *Myths of the Greeks and Romans*. New York: New American Library, 1962.

Harding, M. Esther. *The Way of All Women*. New York: C. G. Jung Foundation, 1970 (first edition, 1933).

———. *Woman's Mysteries: Ancient and Modern*. New York: C. G. Jung Foundation, 1971 (first edition, 1935).

Harms, Valerie, ed. *Celebration with Anaïs Nin*. Greenwich, Conn.: Magic Circle Press, 1973.

Harms, Valerie. *Stars in My Sky: Maria Montessori, Anaïs Nin, Frances Steloff*. Weston, Conn.: Magic Circle Press, 1976.

Hatterer, Lawrence J. "The Woman Artist," *The Artist in Society* New York: Grove Press, 1965.

Hess, Thomas B. and Elizabeth C. Baker. *Art and Sexual Politics.* New York: Macmillan, 1973.

Hinz, Evelyn J. *The Mirror and the Garden: Realism and Reality in the Writings of Anaïs Nin.* Publications Committee of the Ohio State University Libraries, 1971.

———, ed. *The World of Anaïs Nin: Critical and Cultural Perspectives. Mosaic,* Vol. XI, No. 1 (October, 1977).

Horney, Karen. *Self-Analysis.* New York: W. W. Norton & Co., 1942.

Jason, Philip K., ed. *Anaïs Nin Reader.* Chicago: The Swallow Press, Inc., 1973.

Jung, C. G. "Anima and Animus," *Two Essays on Analytical Psychology.* New York: C. G. Jung Foundation.

———. "Approaching the Unconscious," *Man and His Symbols.* Edited by C. G. Jung. New York: Dell, 1968.

———. *Memories, Dreams, Reflections.* Edited by Aniela Jaffé, Translated from the German by Richard and Clara Winston. New York: Random House, 1961.

———. *Psychological Reflections.* Edited by Jolande Jacobi. New York: Harper & Row, 1961.

Jung, Emma. *Animus and Anima: Two Essays.* New York: Analytical Psychology Foundation of New York, 1969.

Kandinsky, Wassily. *Concerning the Spiritual in Art.* Translated from the German by Michael Sadleir. New York: George Wittenborn, Inc., 1947 (first German edition, 1914).

Lippard, Lucy, ed. *Surrealists on Art.* Englewood Cliffs, N.J.: Prentice-Hall, Inc., 1970.

Olsen, Tillie. "Silences," *The Harvard Advocate.* (CVI, No. 2/3, Winter, 1973).

Rank, Otto. *Art and Artist: Creative Urge and Personality Development.* Translated from the German by Charles Francis Atkinson. New York: Agathon Press, 1968 (first English edition, 1932).

———. *Beyond Psychology.* New York: Dover Publications, 1958 (first English edition, 1941).

Rimbaud, Arthur. *Illuminations and Other Prose Poems.* Translated from the French by Louise Varèse. New York: New Directions, 1946 (first French edition, 1866). This volume includes the two "Lettres du Voyant" of 1871.

Schopenhauer, Arthur, *The World as Will and Idea.* Translated from the German by R. B. Haldane and J. Kemp. Garden City, N.Y.: Doubleday and Co., Inc., 1961 (first German edition, 1819).

Shattuck, Roger. "The Art of Stillness," *The Banquet Years: The Origins of the Avant-Garde in France: 1885 to World War I.* Garden City, N.Y.; Doubleday and Co., Inc., 1961.

Sokel, Walter H. *The Writer in Extremis: Expressionism in Twentieth-Century German Literature.* Stanford, Calif., Stanford University Press, 1959.

Spencer, Sharon. "Anaïs Nin: A Heroine for Our Time," *Journal of the Otto Rank Association,* Vol. 11, No. 3, Summer, 1977.

―――. "Femininity and the Woman Writer: Doris Lessing's *The Golden Notebook* and the *Diary* of Anaïs Nin," *Women's Studies* (Vol. 1, No. 3, 1973).

―――. "An Interview with Anaïs Nin," *Shantih: International Writings,* Winter/Spring, 1972.

―――. "Introduction: The Novel as Mobile in Space," *Cities of the Interior,* Anaïs Nin. Chicago: The Swallow Press, Inc., 1947 (first edition, 1959).

―――. *Space, Time and Structure in the Modern Novel.* Chicago, The Swallow Press, Inc., 1974.

Wescher, Herta. *Collage.* Translated from the German by Robert E. Wolf. New York: Harry N. Abrams, 1968.

Woolf, Virginia. *A Room of One's Own.* New York: Harcourt Brace and World, 1929.

Zaller, Robert, ed. *A Casebook on Anaïs Nin.* New York: New American Library, 1974.

Ziolkowski, Theodore. *Hermann Broch.* Columbia Essays on Modern Writers, No. 3. New York: Columbia University Press, 1964.

Index

186